The Real Effects of Credit Line Drawdowns

1 Introduction

During the first year of the financial crisis, the aggregate investment spending of U.S. nonfinancial corporations remained at pre-crisis levels, collapsing only after the failure of Lehman Brothers in September 2008. This fact may be surprising, as the recession that started in December 2007 lowered firms' cash flows, and the unfolding financial crisis reduced aggregate liquidity and the availability of new credit. Theoretical work on credit lines offers one explanation for this pattern. In the presence of liquidity shocks, firms rely on prearranged credit lines to maintain investment spending (Holmström and Tirole, 2000). Consistent with this liquidity insurance role of credit lines, aggregate data show a large increase in credit line drawdowns during the financial crisis (Ivashina and Scharfstein, 2010, Campello, Giambona, Graham, and Harvey, 2011).[1]

In this paper, we use detailed firm-level information on credit line drawdowns to assess the extent to which these drawdowns were used to finance corporate investment and therefore had real effects. Because no comprehensive firm-level dataset on credit line drawdowns is readily available, we collected quarterly data on credit lines from regulatory filings for a sample of about 470 public U.S. companies from 2005:Q4 to 2010:Q4. In the process, we also recorded data on credit line availability—the time-varying credit line portion that is effectively available—which allows us to track these covenant-induced restrictions on credit line limits (Sufi, 2009; Huang, 2010; Acharya, Almeida, Ippolito, and Perez, 2013). Our measure of financing constraints—credit line availability—is the key element of our identification strategy to address the potential endogeneity of drawdowns when assessing their real effects.[2]

Using data from our sample of firms, the upper panel of figure 1 shows the large increase in credit line drawdowns during the financial crisis. This figure exhibits a novel fact: Drawdowns had already increased in the second half of 2007, concurrent with the collapse of the asset-backed commercial paper (ABCP) market and thus about a year earlier than what has been documented in the empirical literature. Drawdowns also increased after the collapse of Bear Stearns in March 2008 and, as previously documented, spiked around the Lehman bankruptcy in September 2008. The amount of drawn credit doubled between the beginning (2007:Q3) and the peak of the crisis (2008:Q4). When financial market stress receded in early 2009, firms started to repay their credit lines. As shown in the lower panel of figure 1, drawdowns increased at the time that corporate investment hovered around its pre-crisis level. This aggregate pattern suggests that corporations

---

[1]Ivashina and Scharfstein (2010) document that large firms drew on credit lines because of uncertainty in the financial sector. Campello, Graham, and Harvey (2010) and Campello, Giambona, Graham, and Harvey (2011) provide survey evidence that severely financially constrained firms relied on credit lines for cash during the recent financial crisis.

[2]Taking a different approach Almeida, Campello, Laranjeira, and Weisbenner (2011) focus on firms with debt that matured in the financial crisis and find that these firms reduced investment more than firms without debt that matured in the financial crisis.

used drawdowns to sustain their capital expenditures, lending additional support to the liquidity insurance hypothesis.

An alternative explanation for credit line drawdowns is that during the crisis firms drew on their credit lines and hoarded the cash due to concerns about future access to funding. For example, Ivashina and Scharfstein (2010) report that executives of very large firms emphasized the "uncertainty about the future of the financial system" as one of the main reasons for increased credit line drawdowns during the crisis. This reasoning suggests that firms may have drawn on their credit lines for precautionary purposes. Figure 2 shows the behavior of corporate cash during the financial crisis. Cash holdings declined during the fall of 2007, increased somewhat in the first half of 2008, and shot up during the collapse of Lehman Brothers. This pattern suggests that nonfinancial corporations reied, at least in part, on cash holdings to smooth liquidity shocks during the crisis and to maintain investment. Cash holdings increased significantly starting in the second half of 2009, concurrent with an aggregate repayment of outstanding credit line balances.

In our first empirical test of the liquidity insurance role of credit lines, we study the relationship between credit line drawdowns and firm-specific and aggregate liquidity shocks. We measure firm-specific liquidity shocks as the quarterly deviations from firms' average cash flow, sales growth, and operating profits over the sample period. Consistent with theoretical work on the use of credit lines, we show that firms increased their credit line usage in response to adverse changes in liquidity. The response is larger during the crisis–that is, when aggregate liquidity is low and other funding sources, such as bond issuance, are scarce.

In our second empirical test of the liquidity insurance role of credit lines, we study the relationship between credit line drawdowns and investment spending. We use fixed effect panel regressions of capital expenditures on past credit line drawdowns and firm controls. We find that credit line drawdowns were used to finance corporate investment. Our fixed effect regression estimates suggest that a one standard deviation increase in the size of drawdowns is associated with a 4 percent increase in average capital expenditures (about 0.06 percent of total assets).

Although we control for investment opportunities and use lagged variables in our regression framework, we still face a potentially important identification challenge; credit line drawdowns may be endogenous. For example, a forward-looking firm may draw funds from their credit lines as a preemptive response to future investment plans. To address this endogeneity concern, our empirical approach builds on previous work on debt covenant-induced corporate financing constraints. More specifically, we exploit the variation in access to credit lines, measured by credit line availability scaled by total assets (the credit line availability ratio), as our instrument for drawdowns. Intuitively, firms with little access to their credit lines cannot rely on drawdowns to finance investment spending. Access to credit lines is determined by debt contract terms. We

3

argue that contract terms that restrict the availability of undrawn funds—typically borrowing-based formulas—are bank-imposed and thus plausibly exogenous to firms' decisions. Therefore, with credit line availability being predetermined, firms have little scope to influence their line availability when exposed to financial shocks. Our data show that a firm placed at the 25th percentile of the credit line availability distribution in our sample can only use about 85 percent of its remaining line, and a firm at the 10th percentile of the distribution can use only 60 percent.

Using an instrumental variable approach, we estimate the effect conditional on firms having access to their credit lines and find that a one standard deviation increase in drawdowns (about 3 percent) is associated with a 9 percent increase in average capital expenditure (approximately 0.13 percent of total assets) during benign times. We find that the effect was larger, a roughly 16 percent increase in capital expenditures, during the financial crisis. This amplification during the crisis is stronger for small firms and firms that do not pay dividends. These firms are usually considered otherwise financially constrained and are hence more likely to rely on credit lines to smooth liquidity shocks.

Our findings are robust to the use of alternative measures of investment (for example, changes in plant, property, and equipment), additional lags for our firm control variables (to better account for persistent effects of idiosyncratic shocks), continuous variables that control for the effect of the financial crisis (e.g., the TED spread, and lending standards from the Senior Loan Officer Opinion Survey, SLOOS), and different splits of our sample of firms (for example, by size, by dividend-paying status, and by bond rating) to account for the role of financing constraints. In complementary cross-sectional regressions, we find that firms with more credit line availability during the pre-crisis period drew down more and used these funds to invest during the financial crisis.

We then explore an alternative explanation for credit line drawdowns during the financial crisis: Firms drew on their credit lines and hoarded the cash because they were concerned that their banks might not be able to honor credit line commitments (Ivashina and Scharfstein, 2010). This explanation suggests that credit line drawdowns during the crisis were precautionary in nature. If these drawdowns were in fact largely precautionary, then firms' cash holdings should increase almost one-to-one with credit line drawdowns. Using the identification strategy discussed above, we do not find evidence that drawdowns differentially increased cash holdings more during the financial crisis than at other times, except for large and investment grade firms. In the cross section, we also find that drawdowns instrumented with pre-crisis availability also reduced cash holdings during the crisis. In sum, our findings suggest that for the majority of firms, drawdowns during the financial crisis did not necessarily reflect concerns about the health of their lenders. We therefore conclude that, with the possible exception of large and investment grade firms, the liquidity insurance motive prevailed over the precautionary hoarding motive during the financial crisis.

4

Our paper is closely related to previous work by Campello, Graham, and Harvey (2010) and Campello, Giambona, Graham, and Harvey (2011), who analyze credit line usage and the real effects of financing constraints during the financial crisis. Unlike these studies, which employ the Chief Financial Officer (CFO) survey data from 2009 and provide evidence of large credit line drawdowns by self-reported financially constrained firms, our paper exploits the panel dimension of our dataset when estimating the effect of drawdowns on investment. Our finding that firms with access to their credit lines use drawdowns for investment purposes is consistent with Chava and Roberts (2008), who use a regression discontinuity around debt covenant violations and show that investment drops after such violations.[3]

Our results also suggest that, at least early in the crisis, banks continued to perform their role as liquidity insurers for nonfinancial firms.[4] The upper panel of figure 3 shows that the total credit line extended to firms in our panel contracted sharply around the Lehman failure. For comparison, the lower panel of figure 3 shows that total bank commercial and industrial (C&I) lending exhibits the same contraction.[5] Cornett et al (2011) and Acharya and Mora (2013) study this credit crunch and find liquidity hoarding by banks mostly in response to the failure of Lehman, which suggests that from the third quarter of 2008, banks may not have been able to continue to function as liquidity insurers for nonfinancial firms.[6]

Our results have important policy implications for bank regulation. Taken together, the evidence presented in our paper highlights the importance of the liquidity insurance provided by banks through credit lines for the real economy, especially in times of low aggregate liquidity. Thus, a potential consequence of bank regulation, either through higher capital charges on credit lines or through liquidity regulation, could be that banks may be less able or willing to provide liquidity insurance to nonfinancial corporations, which, in turn, may reduce aggregate investment and thus amplify the real consequences of liquidity shocks.

The remainder of the paper is organized as follows. Section 2 briefly reviews the literature on credit lines. Section 3 describes the data collection process and presents summary statistics and drawdowns during the sample period. Section 4 assesses the real effects of credit line drawdowns. Section 5 discusses the findings. Section 6 concludes.

---

[3] Falato and Liang (2014) find that debt covenant violations also affect employment.

[4] Kashyap, Rajan, and Stein (2002) and Gatev and Strahan (2006) argue that banks have a natural advantage in the provision of liquidity.

[5] At the same time drawdowns from ABCP back-up lines and anticipated losses in loans and securities holdings led to liquidity-hoarding by banks (Berrospide, 2013).

[6] Chodorow-Reich (2014) finds that the credit retrenchment after the Lehman failure reduced employment.

2 Credit Lines - Theory and Evidence

The theoretical literature emphasizes the ability to insure against revenue or, more generally, liquidity shocks as the key rationale for firms to have prearranged credit lines. Specifically, a firm may need liquidity in states of the world in which it has insufficient cash flows either to continue a current project—for instance, the firm may be unable to pay for intermediate goods or for a wages bill—or to realize new investment opportunities. In such an environment, credit lines can be efficient in providing the required funding (Boot, Thakor, and Udell, 1987; Thakor, 2005). The liquidity management literature suggests that firms do not wait until the liquidity shock occurs to secure the funds to withstand the shock. Instead, the firm may either (i) self-insure by hoarding reserves in the form of cash or liquid securities that can be sold in the face of higher liquidity pressures, or (ii) secure a credit line from a financial institution (Holmström and Tirole, 2000; Tirole, 2006).

This trade-off between cash holdings and credit lines suggests that firms increase their cash holdings relative to their reliance on credit lines when external finance is costly relative to holding cash. Opler, Pinkowitz, Stulz, and Williamson (1999) and Almeida, Campello, and Weisbenner (2004) document that firms are more likely to increase cash balances when access to external finance is limited or costly. Faulkender and Wang (2006) find that the marginal value of cash is larger for financially constrained firms. Denis and Sibilkov (2010) argue that higher cash holdings allow financially constrained firms to realize valuable investment opportunities. Finally, Duchin, Ozbas, and Sensoy (2010) show that firms entering the 2007-2009 financial crisis with low cash balances exhibited a larger drop in investment.

Existing empirical evidence suggests that credit lines are also widely used by firms to manage their liquidity needs. For instance, Shockley and Thakor (1997) document that most U.S. commercial bank lending to corporations is done via bank loan commitments. Thakor (2005) and, more recently, Acharya, Almeida, and Campello (2013) propose models in which a large portion of firms draw on their credit lines simultaneously. For example, in response to an aggregate liquidity shortfall. Thakor (2005) argues that credit lines insure against credit contractions and that overlending may occur in times when debt covenants are not binding. Acharya, Almeida, and Campello point out that the firm's exposure to aggregate liquidity risk is a key determinant of their choice between cash and credit lines. Demiroglu and James (2011) provide a review of the evidence on the importance of credit lines for liquidity management.[7]

---

[7]While most of the evidence in the literature uses U.S. data, Jimienez, Lopez, and Saurina (2009) provide evidence from Spanish firms and reach similar conclusions. The authors also conclude that previous default leads to less credit line use, which may be the result of more-intense bank monitoring. Lins, Servaes, and Tufano (2010) use an international survey to more closely examine international differences in liquidity policies. They find that firms make greater use of credit lines when external credit markets are poorly developed.

More recently, the literature has focused on the determinants of credit line use. Work in this literature studies firm's liquidity management as the interaction between different funding sources at the firm level: cash holdings, debt, and credit lines. Campello, Giambona, Graham, and Harvey (2011) and Campello, Giambona, Graham, and Harvey (2012) use a 2009 CFO survey with responses from 31 countries and find that constrained firms (small, private, non-investment grade, and unprofitable) were more likely to draw on their credit lines in the recent financial crisis. This study, which relies on firm information at two points in time, also concludes that constrained firms faced somewhat less favorable conditions for credit line renewal. Ivanshina and Scharfstein (2010) document a large increase in credit line drawdowns and a cutback of new credit around the collapse of Lehman Brothers.[8] Montoriol-Garriga and Sekeris (2009) exploit the Federal Reserve's Survey of Terms of Business Lending to argue that there was a run on credit lines during the financial crisis. Moreover, Campello, Graham, and Harvey (2010) document that financially constrained firms reduced investment significantly in the financial crisis. Mian and Santos (2011), using data from the Shared National Credit program, also document a cyclical behavior of credit line use and refinancing decisions.

Another strand of the literature examines the limitations of credit lines in their liquidity insurance role. For example, the role of debt covenants in restricting firm access to credit lines has been documented by Sufi (2009); Demiroglu, James, and Kizilaslan (2009); and Huang (2010). Sufi (2009) argues that banks monitor firms' cash flows, which are part of debt covenants that restrict access to credit lines. He shows that credit lines are a liquidity substitute only for high-cash flow firms, as low-cash flow firms face more restricted access to credit lines due to tightened covenants. Demiroglu, James, and Kizilaslan (2009) expand Sufi's sample of publicly listed companies with data on private firms and show that tight credit conditions reduce access to credit lines more for privately held firms. Huang (2010) use data on small businesses and shows that a bank's financial conditions restrict credit line access to small and risky firms.

Acharya, Almeida, Ippolito, and Perez (2013) developed a theoretical framework in which credit lines work as monitored liquidity insurance. Bank monitoring of covenant compliance makes firms use their lines wisely–taking into account future cash flows, borrowing costs, and investment opportunities–as the cost of monitored liquidity insurance increases with liquidity risk. In a similar vein, Sun (2013) proposes a model of the trade-off between cash and credit lines in which access to credit lines is contingent on the banks' ability or willingness to supply the funds. Contingent access to credit lines creates incentives for firms to either reduce leverage to avoid exceeding borrowing limits or to issue long term debt and hoard the cash even though they may not have a real need for it. Cash hoarding then results from financial uncertainty (the possibility of restricted access to

---

[8]Santos (2010), using LPC's DealScan, links credit supply to bank health. Here, credit supply is measured as the loan terms of new credit during and after the crisis.

credit line funding) and occurs because the liquidity insurance cost (fees paid on undrawn funds during uncertainty) may become greater than the cost of borrowing and holding idle cash.

Finally, Chen, Hu, and Mao (2011) and Barakova and Parthasarathy (2012) empirically investigate the liquidity insurance role of credit lines using bank-level data. Both papers find that despite the access limitations, debt covenants do not restrict the liquidity insurance role of credit lines. Chen, Hu, and Mao (2011) find that credit line drawdowns depend on relationship lending and bank reputation issues but that banks did not restrict credit line access severely during the recent crisis. Barakova and Parthasarathy (2012) also show that banks seldom limit access until the firm becomes very risky or overuses its line. As discussed below, we also find that credit line availability was not significantly reduced on average during the crisis (from 90 percent to 86 percent). However, credit availability was significantly constrained for small firms in the lowest percentile of the availability distribution.

Two key hypotheses related to the liquidity insurance role of credit lines that we will subsequently test can be derived from the literature. First, firms draw on their credit lines in the face of revenue or funding shocks and use the proceeds to continue their current operations and to sustain their investment plans. Low aggregate liquidity exacerbate individual (idiosyncratic) shocks and amplify the effect of drawdowns on investment. Second, an alternative hypothesis is that firms hoard the drawn funds as idle cash for precautionary reasons–that is, in anticipation of future funding needs and in the presence of financial uncertainty.

3   Data

This section first describes the sampling methods and data sources. It then discusses the sample properties and provides summary statistics. The section concludes by analyzing firms' credit line drawdown decisions.

3.1   Data Collection Process

We use two main data sources: Standard and Poor's COMPUSTAT and Security and Exchange Commission (SEC) regulatory filings (10-Ks and 10-Qs).[9] Our sample selection criterion for the universe of COMPUSTAT firms is that the firm was in operation in 2005:Q4 and in 2008:Q3 and was not an agricultural, utility, or financial service company. We stratify the remaining firms by industry and size to ensure the representativeness of our sample. We then randomly sample a total of 600 nonfinancial firms in 75 strata. We use the company's name and tax number to obtain the

---

[9]The Standard and Poor's COMPUSTAT data was accessed via WRDS from the University of Pennsylvania.

10-Ks and 10-Qs for each firm from 2005:Q4 to 2010:Q4.

To identify credit line users, we conduct a keyword search in the regulatory filings. Specifically, we search for "credit facility," "credit facilities," "credit line," "credit lines," "line of credit," "lines of credit," "loan facility," "loan facilities," "revolving facility," "term loan," and "term loans." We then read the respective paragraphs to extract the relevant information on credit lines and their use.[10] We exclude bridge facilities, merger facilities, floor plan facilities, and credit lines denominated in foreign currency. Since we focus on revolving credit lines, we exclude term loans that are part of credit line facilities.

The most common interest rates on credit lines are a bank's prime rate or the one- or three-month London Interbank Offered Rate (LIBOR). Margins on LIBOR are higher than margins on prime rates. After the financial crisis, many (re-)negotiated lines include minimum interest rates or LIBOR/prime floors. Firms incur fees on the unused portion of their facility or on the total commitment. Firms may incur a fee if they terminate the agreement prior to the maturity date.

A typical credit line contract includes debt covenants in the form of requirements on maximum leverage, minimum profitability, and quality of collateral (the most common being receivables and inventories). In some cases, there are also material adverse change (MAC) provisions allowing the lender to terminate the loan agreement if the borrower experiences material changes in its financial conditions. These provisions are subject to legal interpretation, and invoking them usually leads to litigation.[11] The most common covenant violations are failure to submit the SEC filings on time; minimum earnings before interest, taxes, depreciation, and amortization (EBITDA) violations; collateral and cash flow violations; and leverage ratio violations. After a covenant violation, firms generally experience an increase in the interest rate margin. However, depending on the relationship with their borrowers, banks may waive the covenant violation and modify the terms and conditions of the credit facility.

After subsequent violations over several quarters, the firm will be forced to either enter into a forbearance agreement and negotiate another line (possibly with another bank) or to stop borrowing from existing credit lines (e.g., through credit line termination and a requirement to repay outstanding balance). In certain situations, although a company does not violate a covenant,

---

[10]Since firms sometimes convert credit line debt into term loans, we found it useful to include "term loan(s)" in the search. We observe that sometimes term loan facilities are not immediately drawn, though most are drawn within the quarter they are received. We also find situations in which firms have a combination of term loans and delayed draw term loans. These latter term loans must usually be drawn within a year of commitment, otherwise the firm pays a commitment fee on the remaining unused portion. In some other cases, the credit agreement is negotiated to include a revolving line and a term loan, while at other times the term loan is added later.

[11]A bank may not invoke MAC provisions when it is in good financial health. However, when needed, a bank may directly influence the volumes of drawdowns by reducing credit availability to borrowers who are not in compliance with covenants or whose collateral has declined in value. For a more comprehensive discussion, see Sufi (2009) and Huang (2010).

the fact that it exceeds a maximum ratio (e.g., leverage) or falls below a minimum ratio (e.g., EBITDA/assets) leads to restrictive covenants that limit their borrowing capacity. We therefore distinguish between unused credit lines (total credit line less amount outstanding) and available credit lines (total credit line less covenant-induced reduction).

A specific example helps clarify the difference between unused and available portions of a credit line. The 2007 10-K of IEC Electronics Corp. states that "IEC has a line of credit with a maximum borrowing limit up to $6.0 million based upon advances on eligible accounts receivable and inventory." Hence, the unused portion is $6 million less the used portion. However, according to IEC's 10-K, the base formula for the available portion is the minimum of (1) $6 million and (2) 0.85*accounts receivable+0.35*inventory. Cash flow and leverage based formulas are also common. In other cases, the available portion is reduced by letters of credit or by the use of commercial paper facilities. It follows that the maximum amount a firm can still draw is the available portion less the used portion. Unused commitments, usually defined as the maximum borrowing limit less the used portion, therefore tend to overstate credit availability to firms.

Our firm-level data extracted from regulatory filings include the total amount of the credit facility, the amount drawn, the remaining unused amount, the amount available, and information on covenant violations and terms of credit described above. Appendix 1 describes in detail the information we extract from footnotes to the firm's financial statements in their SEC regulatory filings. Appendix 2 presents an example to illustrate how we construct our credit line variables (used, unused and available amounts) based on the data from regulatory filings. We complement our database with financial variables from COMPUSTAT. As additional controls in our analysis we add cash, cash and short term investments, credit ratings, long and short term debt measures, shareholder's equity, total assets, total debt, total expenses, total revenue, and working capital.

3.2   Sample Summary Statistics

The use of credit lines is widespread for firms in our sample. Of the original 600 nonfinancial firms in the sample, 467 have a credit line at some point in time. In the remainder of the paper we restrict our attention to these 467 firms. Table 2 provides summary statistics. For the firms in our sample, credit lines are about 17 percent of their assets.[12] Firms with credit lines are on average

---

[12]For comparison, Sufi (2009) reports that 85 percent of firms in his sample have a line of credit between 1996 and 2003, and the lines of credit represent about 16 percent of their assets. Campello, Giambona, Graham, and Harvey (2011) report the following average ratios (as percent of total assets): credit lines of 24 percent, cash holdings of 12 percent, and cash flows of 9 percent, for their sample of 397 U.S. nonfinancial firms based on their 2009 CFO survey. The difference in the cash holdings and cash flow ratios reflects not only the differences between our definitions of cash and cash flows and theirs, but also the fact that our sample covers the financial crisis period, when—as already documented—firms may have boosted their cash holdings and savings from cash flows in anticipation of liquidity pressures.

larger than the average nonfinancial firm in COMPUSTAT. They also tend to have a somewhat higher leverage than the average firm in COMPUSTAT (a debt-to-asset ratio of 0.26 compared with 0.23 for the average firm in COMPUSTAT). The average nonfinancial firm in COMPUSTAT holds 21 percent of assets in cash and cash-like equivalents. Consistent with previous findings on the trade-off between cash and credit lines, the firms with credit lines in our sample hold on average 7 percentage points less cash (14 percent). On balance, firms with credit lines in our sample tend to be more profitable and have higher cash flows than average COMPUSTAT firms. In sum, the properties of our sample and the difference between firms with credit lines and the COMPUSTAT universe are consistent with previous findings reported in the literature.

3.3 Credit Line Drawdowns during the Financial Crisis

We focus our analysis on revolving credit lines, as they are the most common form of bank lending to nonfinancial firms. Revolving lines are the amount that firms can draw down, repay, and continue drawing down for the duration of the facility. Firms rely on these lines to satisfy short term liquidity needs. The upper panel of figure 3 shows the total use of revolving credit lines for all firms in our sample.[13] Firms started to tap their revolving credit lines during the first half of 2007 and continued to increase credit line usage after the beginning of the financial crisis, which started with a panic in short term funding markets (August 2007).[14] Credit line usage (the solid blue line) increased significantly after the Bear Stearns failure in March 2008, spiked after the collapse of Lehman Brothers, and reached its peak during the first quarter of 2009. Credit line usage in our sample increased by about $14 billion, an increase of almost 100 percent, between 2007:Q1 and 2009:Q1. Total revolving lines of credit (dashed red line) followed a similar pattern. They went up by $35 billion during the same period, with almost all of the increase occurring in 2007.[15] While the drawdowns before the Lehman collapse have not been documented before, the spike in usage around the Lehman collapse and the reduction in total lines of credit are consistent with the evidence from aggregate data and new syndicated loans presented in Ivashina and Scharfstein (2010). In total, the drawdowns during the crisis amount to about 11 percent of the 2007:Q2 unused commitments.

The size of aggregate drawdowns during the crisis suggests that many firms relied on their credit

---

[13] We exclude four companies. Anadarko Petroleum Corporation, First Data Management, and ConocoPhillips have large bridge loan facilities because merger and acquisition activities. Alltel was the target of a leveraged buyout (LBO).

[14] One possibility is that most of the increase in credit line usage is driven by firms that use their credit lines to back up the issuance of commercial paper. However, we do not find evidence that this behavior is driven by the 32 commercial paper-issuing firms in our sample. In fact, we find no difference between firms with commercial paper back-up lines of credit and all other firms in the sample.

[15] Perhaps surprisingly, the Lehman failure was not followed by large credit line cancelations. We find, however, that the Lehman share in syndicated loans was typically not taken up by another bank in the syndicate, which reduced total revolving lines somewhat.

lines to weather the financial crisis. As discussed in section 2, depending on the size of their cash holdings, firms may opt to withstand the effects of a liquidity shock using their cash (cash-rich firms) or by drawing down funds from their credit lines (cash-poor firms). To shed light on which firms contribute most to the aggregate cash holding and credit line drawdown behavior, we split our sample into firms that entered the financial crisis with low and high cash holdings. Low-cash (high-cash) firms have an average *Cash/TA* ratio during the pre-crisis period (between 2005:Q1 and 2007:Q2) lower than (greater than) the aggregate average *Cash/TA* ratio during the pre-crisis period. As shown in the upper panel of figure 4, high-cash firms (dashed red line) significantly reduced their cash holdings at the onset of the financial crisis–that is, immediately after the collapse of the ABCP market in August 2007. These cash-rich firms were indeed weathering the financial crisis using their cash. However, both types of firms increased their cash holdings only after the first half of 2009.

The lower panel of figure 4 plots average credit line usage by firm type. High-cash firms increased their credit line use as ABCP markets came under stress. Low-cash firms (dotted blue line) were apparently untouched by the collapse of the ABCP market and gradually increased their cash holdings during the crisis. As expected, these firms rely heavily on committed credit lines. Low-cash firms started to draw down their credit lines only in 2008, particularly after the Bear Sterns failure in March, and even more after the collapse of Lehman Brothers in September. When financial market stress receded, high-cash firms maintained their credit line usage whereas low-cash firms started to repay their credit lines. Thus, figure 4 provides suggestive evidence that both high- and low-cash firms drew on their credit lines during the financial crisis but did so at different times and paces. Furthermore, neither appears to have done so to significantly increase cash holdings.

One alternative to draw on credit lines is to issue bonds. The top panel of figure 6 plots corporate bond issuances for all nonfinancial firms reported in Bloomberg. In the aggregate, bond issuance dropped significantly from 2007:Q2 to 2008:Q4 especially for speculative grade firms. First Data Corp's issuance of $6 billion LBO bonds accounts for almost all speculative grade issuances in the U.S. in 2008:Q3.[16] Furthermore, there were essentially no speculative grade issuances in the aftermath of the Lehman failure. Similarly, investment grade firms did not increase bond issuance early in the crisis. In the second half of 2008, issuances by investment grade firms dropped significantly. While bond issuance recovered in 2009, the spike in bond issuance in 2009:Q1 shown in the figure needs to be assessed with caution as it is driven by few investment grade firms with very large issuances.[17] The bottom panel of figure 6 plots corporate bond issuances for firms in our sample. Bond issuances appear to be low compared to the full sample in 2006; however, in all other years, bond issuance for firms in our sample mimics that for firms in the full sample. Bond

---

[16]We do not find that the firms in our sample were engaged in significant private placements under rule 144(a).

[17]Roche, for instance, raised some $30 billion from bond issuances in that quarter.

issuance dropped with the start of the financial crisis and recovered only in 2009. In sum, the bond issuance patterns suggest that bond issuances were not a substitute for credit line drawdowns or, more generally, for bank credit during the financial crisis, perhaps because bond spreads had already increased as well.

Despite the significant increase in credit line drawdowns observed on aggregate during the financial crisis, a cross-firm analysis of our data shows that not all firms had full access to their credit lines because, for some firms, debt covenants reduced the credit amount that was available to them. Figure 5 plots average credit line use and availability, measured as a percent of total revolving lines, over our sample period. The percentage of credit line used (dashed red line) mimics the drawdown pattern documented in the upper panel of figure 1. Average credit line availability (solid blue line) is about 90 percent at the beginning of the sample. It declines early in the crisis, recovers, and then falls again in the wake of the Lehman failure. Only toward the end of the sample does average credit line availability recover to close to pre-crisis levels. Plotting the percentile of the credit line availability distribution, figure 5 shows that the lower percentiles of the distribution dropped during the crisis. These drops indicate that an increasing number of firms experienced reduced access to their credit lines.

3.4   Determinants of Credit Line Drawdowns

The first key prediction of the insurance theory of credit lines is that firms draw on credit lines after experiencing an adverse liquidity shock. To assess which variables determine credit line drawdowns, we employ two measures of drawdown. First, we use an indicator variable that is equal to 1 if credit line usage—the amount outstanding—increased from the previous to the present quarter and 0 otherwise. Second, we measure the drawdown size as the change in the credit line amount outstanding from the previous to the present quarter scaled by the previous quarter's total assets. We use the following baseline regression framework:

$$
Drawdown_{i,t} = c_i + \tau_t + \beta_1 \; liquidity \; shock_{i,t-1} + \beta_2 \; liquidity \; shock_{i,t-1} \times crisis_t + \gamma \cdot X_{i,t-1} + \epsilon_{i,t}. \tag{1}
$$

In the first set of regressions, our dependent variable, $Drawdown$, refers to a dummy variable that is equal to 1 in a quarter in which a firm increased its credit line usage. We employ binary discrete-choice models (fixed effects panel logit models) in our estimation. As in Holmström and Tirole (1998), the $liquidity\; shock$ admits several interpretations, such as a shortfall in the firm's revenues or its net worth, which determines its financing capacity. We use three different forms

13

of idiosyncratic liquidity shocks, each measured as deviations in a firm's revenues and cash flows relative to their mean. These firm-level shocks include shocks to sales growth, the operating-income-to-total assets ratio, and the cash-flow-to-total assets ratio. We also include a crisis dummy variable that is equal to 1 for the quarters from 2007:Q3 to 2008:Q4 (from the collapse of ABCP market to the Troubled Asset Relief Program (TARP)) to reflect the squeeze in the interbank market. Since we are using firm fixed effects, the identification of the coefficient is driven by within-firm variation. Hence, our interpretation of the coefficients on sales growth, the operating-income-to-total assets ratio, and the-cash flow-to-total assets ratio as idiosyncratic shocks is plausible. The controls, $X_{i,t-1}$, include size measured as the log of total assets, a modified Altman Z-score, the tangible assets-to-total assets ratio, the market-to-book ratio, a dummy indicating whether the market-to-book ratio is greater than or equal than 8, cash flow volatility, used credit line to available credit line ratio, and leverage.

Theory suggests that a shock to the firm's revenues—e.g. to sales growth—increases the probability of a credit line drawdown. We therefore expect β_1 to be negative and significant. Consistent with our hypothesis, columns 1 through 3 in the upper panel of table 3 show that the coefficient of our three measures of a firm's liquidity shocks has a strong negative effect on credit line drawdowns when drawdowns are measured by the dummy variable.[18] Next, we include interaction terms of *liquidity shock* and *crisis* to assess whether firms are more likely to draw on their lines when aggregate liquidity is low and other sources of financing are less available. Hence, we expect the coefficient on the interaction term β_2 to be negative and significant. While all point estimates for the three interaction terms are negative, as shown in columns 4 through 6, only the interaction term of shocks to operating income and the crisis dummy is statistically significant.

In the second set of regressions, our dependent variable, *Drawdown*, refers to the drawdown size relative to total assets. Drawdown size is measured as the quarterly change in the dollar amount of credit line use. Note that in this specification, repayments show up as negative drawdowns. Columns 1 through 3 in the lower panel of table 3 show that our measures of idiosyncratic shocks have a strong negative effect on the size of credit line drawdowns. Columns 4 through 6 show that the interaction terms of *liquidity shock* and the *crisis* dummy are also negative and significant, suggesting that firms drew considerably larger amounts from their credit lines during the crisis following a shortfall in their cash flows, operating income, and sales growth.

---

[18]Firms that have a credit line but never drew on it during the sample period lack sufficient variation when we use the fixed effect logit panel regression. Hence, these regressions exclude 125 firms that did not draw on their credit lines during the sample period. Only firms that exhibited a drawdown at any point in time are included in these regressions. For robustness, we used random effect logit panel regressions, which also include the firms that have credit lines but chose not to draw on them during the sample period. The coefficients in the random effect models are larger in part because they exploit the variation between firms that draw on their lines and those that never do (not reported here). Using a random-effect probit model yields similar results.

In sum, our findings are consistent with the insurance hypothesis of credit lines. Firms draw on their credit lines in response to adverse liquidity shocks, and the response is larger during times of low aggregate liquidity when few other funding options are available. The findings also suggest that banks fulfilled their role as liquidity providers to nonfinancial firms during the crisis.

4 Real Effects of Credit Line Drawdowns

In this section we assess the real effects of credit lines. We first estimate the baseline specification and then account for the likely endogeneity of credit line drawdowns. Next, we conduct a series of robustness tests. Last, we assess whether credit line drawdowns during the crisis increased cash holdings.

4.1 Drawdowns Finance Investment

We now turn our attention to the purpose of credit line drawdowns. The second key prediction of the liquidity insurance hypothesis is that firms use credit line drawdows to finance investment or current operations. Hence, credit line drawdowns should have real effects. In general, investment activities depend on investment opportunities and on the ability to capitalize on them. A positive association of credit line drawdowns with investment therefore indicates that the ability to draw on credit lines *facilitates* investment when the opportunity arises.

The top panel of figure 8 shows precisely that credit line drawdowns help facilitate investment plans. The figure presents the capital expenditure to total asset ratio (Capex/TA) in the current quarter for firms that drew on their credit lines in the previous quarter (dashed blue line) and for firms that, having a credit line, did not draw funds from those lines in the previous quarter (long-dashed red line). As a first pass in support of the liquidity insurance hypothesis, this figure illustrates that firms that drew down in the previous quarter invest more in the current quarter than no-drawdown firms. Appendix 2 lists two specific examples that illustrate that firms use credit line drawdowns to finance investment.

Over the sample period firms that draw down their credit lines invest more than firms that have a credit line but do not draw funds from their lines. The average capital expenditure to total assets ratio for firms that drew down their lines during the financial crisis, from 2007:Q3 to 2008:Q4, remained almost constant at about 1.8 percent, compared to the 1.4 percent ratio for firms that did not draw down from their credit lines. Of course, the average Capex/TA ratio for all firms dropped sharply at the peak of the financial crisis in 2008:Q4 and remained around 1.3 percent for drawdown firms and less than 1 percent for no-drawdown firms until 2010:Q4. This pattern of investment is not specific to our sample of firms but holds for all firms in the COMPUSTAT universe. A possible explanation for this pattern is that the decrease in output in late 2007 and early 2008 surprised most market participants. In fact, the National Bureau of Economic Research (NBER) Business Cycle Dating Committee announced that the recession started in December 2007 only in December 2008, when policy interventions such as TARP were reducing the TED spread to pre-crisis levels.[19] The upper panel of figure 8, together with the drawdown behavior documented above (shown in figure 3), illustrates our first piece of evidence on the real effects of credit line drawdowns. This evidence suggests that firms may have used their credit lines to maintain their investment spending and only adjusted their investment plans after the severity of the recession became clear.[20]

To formally test for a positive and causal association between drawdowns and investment in the data, we start our analysis using the panel dimension of our data. We specify the following panel regression:

$$Investment_{i,t} = c_i + \tau_t + \beta_1 \cdot drawdown_{i,t-1} + \beta_2 \cdot drawdown_{i,t-1} \times crisis_t + \gamma \cdot X_{i,t-1} + \epsilon_{i,t}. \tag{2}$$

where $Investment$ is defined as the ratio of capital expenditures to total assets. As in section 3.4, $drawdown$ in specification (2) refers to the size of the drawdown relative to total assets. Since credit lines work as liquidity insurance, we expect the coefficient on drawdown, β_1, to be positive and significant. To assess whether the effects are larger in times of low aggregate liquidity, we also add an interaction term between drawdowns and the crisis dummy variable. We expect the coefficient on the interaction term β_2 to be positive and significant. As additional control variables in $X_{i,t-1}$, we include market-to-book ratio, sales growth, and the operating-profit-to-total assets ratio as a proxy for investment opportunities. We also include size measured as the log of total assets, the cash flow-to-total assets ratio, tangible assets-to-total assets ratio, a dummy for whether the market-to-book ratio is greater than or equal to 8, the Z-score, cash flow volatility, and leverage as additional control variables.

Table 4, columns 1 and 2, report our fixed effect regression estimates of equation (2). The effect of past drawdowns on capital expenditure is large, positive, and significant, suggesting that credit line drawdowns increase capital expenditures.[21] To provide the economic significance of our results, we consider an increase in the size of drawdowns equal to one standard deviation (about 3 percent). Our estimated coefficient of 0.019 indicates that, as a result of this change in drawdowns,

---

[19]For more information on the Business Cycle Dating Committee, see the NBER website at http://www.nber.org/cycles/dec2008.html.

[20]Another possible explanation is the presence of large adjustment costs for capital expenditures.

[21]In unreported regressions, we also use current drawdowns and find similar results.

the average capital expenditure as a percent of total assets increases by about 0.06 percent (0.019 x 0.03). Taking into account that the average capital expenditure ratio for firms that have credit lines in our sample is 1.3 percent of total assets, the predicted change in drawdowns is associated with an increase in capital expenditures of about 4 percent (0.0006/0.013). The interaction of drawdowns and the crisis dummy is negative but insignificant, suggesting that the effect on investment is not amplified by the financial crisis.

4.2 Endogeneity of Drawdowns

While lagging our drawdown variable alleviates simultaneity concerns, drawdowns may still be endogenous. For instance, a firm may decide to draw on their credit line after experiencing an adverse liquidity shock, foreseeing the need for additional liquidity to finance capital expenditures. We therefore extend our fixed effect regression and employ an instrumental variable panel approach to deal with the endogeneity problem.

Our identification approach builds on previous work that highlights the role of financing constraints. We use a particular institutional feature of credit line contracts and instrument drawdowns with a measure of the extent to which a firm is financially constrained given by credit line availability. Credit line availability is predetermined by the contract terms of the credit facility and thus reflects lender requirements, which in many cases are out of the firm's control or exceed its bargaining power. Credit availability reflects credit supply factors and a type of financing constraint. Thus, we define our instrument as the availability ratio, measured as credit line availability over total assets. This definition means that we estimate the effect of credit line drawdowns conditional on firms having access to their credit lines and hence a positive relationship, while the literature more commonly estimates the effect conditional on the firm being constrained. As such, our definition is related to Chava and Roberts (2008), who identify financing constraints as situations when firms breach contract covenants. In comparison, our measure includes contractually defined automatic reductions in the firms' debt capacity, which are, in general, not waived.

First, we show that our instrument exhibits enough sample variation to identify the real effect of credit line drawdowns. Figure 7 shows the percentiles of credit line availability throughout the sample period. There is not only significant variation in the cross section of firms but also within firms over time. The firm-level standard deviation of the availability ratio shows that there is a considerable amount of variation on the firm level that we are exploiting in our identification strategy. Furthermore, the median firm in our sample has almost full credit line availability. We control for this situation by using an indicator variable for whether a firm has a ratio of 1—that is, the firm faces no constraints when accessing the credit line.

Another variable associated with the credit line contract that we employ is the firm's remaining debt capacity on the credit line. We control for remaining debt capacity with the ratio of used credit line to credit line availability during the previous quarter, taking into account again that the credit line availability depends on predetermined contract terms. With the possible exception of commercial back-up lines, reductions in the firm's remaining debt capacity is beyond a firm's direct control, as they relate to collateral or cash flow requirements that are often violated because of lower-than-expected sales. A key identification assumption in this measure is that the availability ratio in $t-2$ is exogenous to capital expenditures in t and only affects capital expenditures in t through drawdowns in $t-1$. In fact, when checking for the validity of our instrumental variable, we find that the availability ratio in $t-2$ has a low correlation with capital expenditures scaled by total assets in t (the correlation coefficient is -0.08). Thus, the availability ratio in $t-2$ is a crucial determinant for the size of credit line drawdowns in $t-1$. Furthermore, we separately control for overall debt capacity by including overall leverage in our main regression. Sargan-Hansen tests confirm that we use valid instruments.

Columns 3 and 4 in table 4 report our results using the instrumental variable regression. The coefficient on drawdowns more than doubles relative to our fixed effect panel regression. A one standard deviation increase in drawdowns is associated with an 9 percent increase in capital expenditures (an increase of 0.13 percent of total assets). This finding supports the liquidity insurance hypothesis of credit lines.[22] Compared with the estimates in column (2), and after we control for the endogeneity of drawdowns, our results suggest that the effect of drawdowns on average capital expenditure increased to 16 percent during the crisis, implying an amplification of about 70 percent, as shown by the positive and significant coefficient of the interaction of drawdowns and the crisis dummy.[23] Thus, firms appear to have used their drawdowns to keep up with their investment plans during the financial crisis.

4.3   Robustness of the Effect of Drawdowns on Investment

We conduct a series of additional tests to assess the robustness of our main result on the real effects of credit line drawdowns. We start by providing cross-sectional evidence to support the validity of our empirical approach and our identification strategy. We calculate the total cumulative credit line drawdown and total investment expenditure during the crisis–that is, over the 2007:Q3-2008:Q3 period–divided by average total assets and then specify the following cross-sectional regression,

$$Investment_{i,crisis} = c + \alpha \cdot drawdown_{i,crisis} + \gamma \cdot X_{i,pre-crisis} + \epsilon_{i,crisis}. \qquad (3)$$

---

[22] In complementary, unreported regressions, we only considered positive drawdowns and found similar results. We also tested whether drawdowns are used to finance inventories. We cannot confirm a positive association between drawdowns and inventories.

[23] Although the coefficient of drawdowns in column (4) is not significant, the sum of that coefficient and the coefficient on the interaction between drawdowns and crisis is positive and significant at the 5 percent level.

18

We also include additional control variables, all averaged over the pre-crisis period (2005:Q4-2007:Q2). The controls include size measured as the log of total assets, the cash-flow-to-total assets ratio, the tangible-assets-to-total assets ratio, a dummy for whether the market-to-book ratio is greater than or equal to 8, the Z-score, cash flow volatility, and leverage. Table 5 presents the results of estimating equation (3). Column 1 shows that the coefficient on cumulative credit line drawdowns during the crisis period is positive and significant. Our results suggest that a one percentage point increase in drawdowns increases capital expenditures by about 28 percentage points during the crisis. To tighten identification, we also instrument cumulative crisis drawdowns by pre-crisis credit line availability. Column 2 shows the result of the IV first stage regression. We find a positive and significant effect of pre-crisis availability on credit line drawdowns, which suggests that firms whose access to their credit lines was less constrained drew more on their credit lines during the crisis. Column 3 shows the result of equation (3) with crisis drawdowns instrumented by pre-crisis availability. The coefficient is positive and significant, implying that a one percentage point increase in instrumented drawdowns increased the capital expenditure ratio during the crisis by 70 percentage points, more than doubling the fixed effect point estimate. This result provides additional support to our finding that access to credit lines played a crucial role in maintaining investment expenditures during the crisis.

One potential concern with our panel approach is that the persistence of shocks may affect the validity of our instruments. For instance, lower-than-expected sales four quarters ago could affect both past credit line availability through lower receivables and investment in the current quarter. To assess whether such persistence affects our result and choice of instrument, we allow for a richer lag structure and include four lags of most control variables. Table 6 shows that the results with additional lags slightly increase the coefficients of drawdowns in our baseline specification.[24]

We also use a different measure of investment in our panel regressions: changes in property, plant, and equipment plus depreciation (PPE). This variable measures the change in long term assets as another proxy for the firm's investment spending.[25] Using changes in PPE as the dependent variable, we find comparable IV regression results to the ones reported for capital expenditures (table 7).

We also conduct additional robustness checks in our panel specifications to better account for macroeconomic effects. We replace our crisis dummy with two continuous measures of aggregate shocks: (a) the average quarterly TED spread and (b) the fraction of banks tightening their lending standards, as reported in the Federal Reserve's Senior Loan Officer Opinion Survey (SLOOS). For

---

[24]We allowed for up to six lags and found similar results.

[25]Unlike our cash flow measure in our baseline specification, Capex/TA, the change in PPE includes non-cash investment activities.

brevity, we only report the selected results on capital expenditures for the full sample and succinctly discuss findings for the subsample. As table 8 shows, using the TED spread or the SLOOS does not change the results. The interaction terms with lending standards measured by the SLOOS variable indicate even stronger effects of credit line drawdowns on capital expenditures during the crisis. Hence, our results are robust to using continuous measures of economic activity.

We expect the effects of credit line drawdowns on investment to be largest for the most financially constrained firms, which have few options but to rely the most on credit lines to smooth financial shocks. We therefore split the sample by commonly used proxies for financing constraints: (1) dividend-paying status, (2) size (small and large firms), and (3) bond ratings (investment grade, high yield, and no rating firms). For the ease of comparison with the results in our baseline specification in section 4.1, we calculate the economic significance of the subsample estimates using a change in drawdowns equivalent to one standard deviation of drawdowns for the average firm in the sample (about 3 percent).

Table 9 shows the regression results of equation (2) by dividend-paying status. Our definition of a dividend-paying firm is a firm that paid at least one positive dividend during the sample period. The top panel shows the regression results for firms that never paid dividends (e.g., more financially constrained). Although our fixed effect panel estimates show that drawdowns are a significant determinant of investment for these firms, in the IV regressions the effect of drawdowns on investment is significant only during the crisis. This result confirms that during times of tight liquidity, more constrained firms are forced to rely more on their credit lines. Our IV regression estimates for these firms suggest that a one standard deviation increase in drawdowns is associated with a 17 percent increase in average capital expenditures (an increase of 0.22 percent of total assets).[26] The results for dividend-paying firms—that is, the less financially constrained firms— are shown in the bottom panel of table 9. We find positive and larger effects of drawdowns on investment in the IV regression (columns 3 and 4). The effect of drawdowns on investment are always significant and increases remarkably during the crisis period. For less financially constrained firms, a one standard deviation increase in drawdowns is associated with about a 13 percent increase in average capital expenditures (about 0.18 percent of total assets). The effect is amplified to 17 percent (about 0.24 percent of total assets) during the crisis.

Next, we analyze differences by firm size. Small and large firms are those in the lower and upper tercile of the size distribution, respectively. Table 10 shows the regression results of equation (2) for the two size subsamples. Consistent with the previous results, columns 3 and 4 in table 10 shows that drawdowns for small firms are important only during the crisis. A one standard deviation increase in drawdowns raises their average capital expenditure by about 12 percent (0.12 percent of

---

[26]Although the coefficient on drawdowns in column (4) is not significant, the sum of that coefficient and the coefficient on the interaction between drawdowns and crisis is positive and significant at the 5 percent level.

total assets). The effect of drawdowns is bigger for large firms (about 12 percent as well), though it does not seem to be amplified by the crisis.

Finally, we split our sample by bond rating. Investment grade, high yield, and no rating firms have a bond rating greater than or equal to BBB, below BBB, or have no bond ratings, respectively. Table 11 shows the regression results of equation (2) for the three bond rating subsamples. The results for no bond rating firms are comparable to those of small firms and firms that never paid dividends. For these firms, the effect of credit line drawdowns are significant for investment (about 13 percent increase in average capital expenditure) only during the crisis. For high yield firms, we find a strong positive effect of drawdowns on investment (about 23 percent increase). The effect is amplified during the crisis (about 33 percent in average capital expenditure). For investment grade firms, which tend to be larger and less financially constrained, we find no effect of drawdowns on capital expenditures. However, we attribute this somewhat counterintuitive result (i.e., it is less consistent with our previous findings when we split firms by size and dividend status) to the fact that we only have about 870 observations for investment grade firms.

In sum, using different subsamples, we find that the real effects of credit line drawdowns on investment are robust to different ways of measuring investment, different proxies for aggregate shocks during the crisis, and different subsamples of firms that account for the role of financial constraints.

4.4   Cash Hoarding during the Crisis

So far we have focused on the predictions of the insurance theory of credit lines. We now turn to an alternative reason for the increased used of credit lines during the crisis. Anecdotal evidence from the financial crisis suggests that firms drew on their credit lines for precautionary reasons (Ivanshina and Scharfstein, 2010). However, the aggregate figures in our sample cast doubt on large (precautionary) cash hoarding during the financial crisis. The bottom panel of figure 8 shows the average cash holdings (Cash/TA) for firms that drew on their credit lines (shaded blue line) and for firms that, having a credit line, did not draw on their lines. This figure shows that average cash holdings of drawdown firms increased a bit at the onset of the crisis but declined in March 2008 (after the failure of Bear Sterns) and remained relatively constant during the financial crisis. Perhaps surprisingly, the cash holdings for these firms only increased strongly after 2009:Q1. Average Cash/TA for no-drawdown firms was higher than for drawdown firms, and it also increased notably only after 2009:Q2. While the average cash holdings could cover up heterogeneity with respect to the firms' overall financial situations, the median cash holdings remained at pre-crisis levels until early 2009 and then increased considerably as well. This pattern suggests that precautionary cash hoarding was not the main reason for the credit line drawdowns during the financial crisis. In fact, cash balances only increased for firms that drew down their credit lines when outstanding credit line debt was being paid off.

We formally test the precautionary cash hoarding hypothesis by assessing whether drawdowns in period $t - 1$ increase cash holdings in period t differently during the crisis. We therefore use the cash-to-total-asset ratio as a dependent variable and assess whether during the crisis more of the previous period's drawdown was held in cash in the period. Hence, the key variable of interest in this specification is the interaction between *Drawdown* and the *crisis* dummy variable. Positive coefficients on the interaction would be consistent with precautionary cash hoarding.

Table 12 shows the results of equation (2), the panel regression, with cash as the dependent variable. In columns 1 and 2, our estimates suggest no effect of drawdown on firm cash holdings. However, after we correct for the endogeneity of drawdowns, our IV regression estimates in columns 3 and 4 show that drawdowns are generally associated with smaller cash holdings. The negative and significant coefficient on drawdowns suggests that a one standard deviation increase in drawdowns reduces average cash holdings by about 1 percent (-0.348 x 0.03) of total assets. Taking into account that the average cash-to-total-asset ratio in our sample is about 12 percent, the increase in drawdowns reduce cash holdings by about 8 percent (-0.01 / 0.12). The positive and significant interaction term of drawdown and the crisis dummy suggests that the reduction in cash holdings was partly mitigated during the crisis (the reduction in cash holdings is then 5 percent). This evidence is consistent with the behavior shown in figure 4, which we interpret as suggesting that the use of cash holdings was complementary to credit line drawdowns in coping with the effects of the crisis and, most likely, in sustaining capital expenditures.

4.5 Robustness of the Effect of Drawdowns on Cash Holdings

We conduct a series of robustness checks to further explore the cash hoarding hypothesis. Again, we start with a validation of our results in the cross section. Table 13 shows the results of equation (3) with changes in cash holdings over the crisis period as the dependent variable. Column 1 confirms the negative relationship between pre-crisis drawdowns and changes in cash holdings in the crisis period. The IV regression estimates in column 3 show a much stronger negative coefficient on drawdowns and suggest a relatively large reduction in cash holdings during the crisis. This finding is consistent with figure 8, which shows decreasing cash holdings during the crisis.

Table 14 shows that alternative macro variables to control for aggregate liquidity shocks such as the TED spread or the tightening of lending standards in SLOOS do not amplify the effect of drawdowns on cash holdings (interactions of drawdowns and the TED spread or SLOOS are positive but insignificant). Adding the interaction terms to the main regression specification in table 12 results in an insignificant point estimate for drawdowns in the IV regressions.

22

When we split the sample by dividend-paying status to account for financing constraints (table 15), we also find that drawdowns are associated with negative cash holdings for firms that never paid dividends (about 9 percent lower cash holdings for a one standard deviation increase in drawdowns). We find some evidence of cash hoarding for dividend-paying firms (that is, less financially constrained firms). For these firms, the positive and significant coefficient on drawdowns suggests that the positive change in drawdowns leads to about a 5 percent increase in average cash holdings. However, this effect was not significant during the crisis.

Table 16 presents the results on cash holdings by firm size. Consistent with previous results on less financially constrained firms, we find that large firms increase their cash holdings with proceeds from credit line drawdowns. The positive and significant coefficient on drawdowns suggests that large firms increase their average cash holdings by about 7 percent as a result of a one standard deviation increase in drawdowns. This effect is amplified to about 10 percent of higher cash holdings during the crisis.[27] However, smaller firms, which tend to be more financially constrained, decreased their cash holdings by about 8 percent (about 1.4 percent of total assets) as a result of larger drawdowns.

Finally, we split the sample by bond ratings. Columns 3 and 4 in table 17 show evidence of cash hoarding for investment grade firms. For these firms, a one standard deviation increase in drawdowns is associated with a 14 percent increase in cash holdings. The effect is more pronounced–about 20 percent–during the crisis. We do not find evidence of cash hoarding resulting from drawdowns for high yield firms. No bond rating firms that drew on their credit lines reduced their cash holdings by about 6 percent as a result of larger drawdowns. For these latter firms, we only find a weak mitigation of the impact of larger drawdowns on cash holdings during the crisis.

In sum, in this section we find a robust negative effect of drawdowns on cash holdings for smaller and more financially constrained firms, which is somewhat mitigated during the crisis. We also find some evidence of cash hording for investment grade firms.

5 Discussion of results

This section puts together our results in testing both the real effect and the cash hoarding hypotheses. Overall, our findings on the real effect hypothesis indicate that firms use credit line drawdowns to maintain their investment spending after adverse idiosyncratic shocks to their revenue and cash flows. When addressing the potential endogeneity of drawdowns by conditioning on access to credit lines—credit line availability—we find positive and significant real effect of drawdowns

---

[27]Although the coefficient on drawdowns in column (4) is not significant, the sum of that coefficient and the coefficient on the interaction between drawdowns and crisis is positive and significant at the 5 percent level.

(about 9 percent increase in average capital expenditures), which seems to be amplified during the financial crisis (to about 16 percent on average). In other words, firms with more availability were able to use their credit lines to maintain their investment spending during times of low aggregate liquidity. In comparison to the findings in the literature on financing constraints, our estimates are conditional on firms having credit lines but facing restricted access to them, rather than firms being constrained and unable to secure a credit line. Covenant-induced restrictions on the use of credit lines therefore imply smaller investment spending financed by drawdowns. Thus, the magnitude of our estimated effect is comparable to the 13 percent decline in investment after debt covenant violations in Chava and Roberts (2008). Our findings are then consistent with the view that financing constraints affect investment by restricting the access to credit line usage (Sufi, 2009; Demiroglu, James, and Kizilaslan, 2009; and Huang, 2010).

Our results using different subsamples confirm that the real effects of credit line drawdowns on investment seem robust to different ways to measure investment, different proxies for aggregate shocks during the crisis, and different subsamples of firms to account for the role of financial constraints. All robustness checks confirm the large effects of drawdowns on investment and the considerable amplification of this effect during the crisis, particularly for smaller and more financially-constrained firms. These findings emphasize the importance of financing constraints and are consistent with Duchin, Ozbas, and Sensoy (2010), who find larger declines in investment for firms that are financially constrained. Unlike these authors who measure financing constraints as low cash reserves or high net short term debt, in this paper we focus on size, dividend-paying status and bond ratings. Our panel evidence complements Campello, Graham, and Harvey (2010) and Campello, Giambona, Graham, and Harvey (2011), who use a survey of CFOs and find that that especially financially constrained firms relied on credit lines for cash and cut investment when credit was not available during the recent financial crisis.

On the cash hoarding hypothesis, our findings suggest that, in the aggregate, credit line drawdowns are associated with a reduction in cash holdings. After splitting our sample by common proxies for financing constraints, we find evidence that the negative effect of drawdowns on cash is more pronounced for small firms, those that never paid dividends, and firms with no bond ratings. We interpret these results as indicating that on average, smaller and more financially constrained firms were already "burning their cash" at times when they drew on their credit lines, though the effect was somewhat mitigated by the financial crisis. Finally, we find some evidence of cash hoarding for a group of investment grade firms. These latter results are consistent with the anecdotal evidence in Ivashina and Scharfstein (2011) and the view that only large and investment grade firms, likely in response to uncertainty about the financial health of their lenders, increased drawdowns and hoarded the cash.

6 Conclusion

Using a unique dataset, we document that credit line drawdowns had already increased in 2007, when disruptions in bank funding markets began to squeeze aggregate liquidity. This finding suggests that banks continued to provide liquidity to firms during the financial crisis. However, this realization of banks' off-balance-sheet risk put additional pressure on banks, even though debt covenants can reduce firms' access to credit lines.

We exploit this variation in access to credit lines across firms as an institutional characteristic of credit line contracts to instrument for the size of the drawdowns. Our key finding is that there are real effects associated with the use of credit lines. We show that firms use their drawdowns to finance investment, thereby providing empirical evidence that credit lines work as liquidity insurance that allows corporations to keep up with their investment plans during times of financial stress. This situation seems to be particularly relevant in an environment in which other funding sources, such as market debt, are not available. The effects of credit line drawdowns on investment are economically large and statistically significant. A one standard deviation increase in the size of the drawdown is associated with a 9 percent increase in average capital expenditures (an increase of 0.13 percent of total assets). The financial crisis amplified the effect of drawdowns on investment significantly. The effect of drawdowns on investment increases by about 70 percent in the full sample–that is, to 16 percent–especially for smaller and financially constrained firms. We find some evidence that firms drew on their lines to increase (precautionary) cash holdings during the crisis only for large and investment grade firms.

References

[1] Acharya, Viral V., Heitor Almeida, and Murillo Campello. 2013. "Aggregate Risk and the Choice between Cash and Lines of Credit." *Journal of Finance* Vol. 68(5), pp. 2059-2116.

[2] Acharya, Viral V., Heitor Almeida, Filippo Ippolito and Ander Perez. 2013. "Credit Lines as Monitored Liquidity Insurance: Theory and Evidence." NBER Working Paper 18892.

[3] Acharya, Viral V. and Nada Mora. 2013. "A Crisis of Banks as Liquidity Providers." *Journal of Finance*, forthcoming.

[4] Almeida, Heitor, Murillo Campello, Bruno Laranjeira, and Scott Weisbenner. 2012. "Corporate Debt Maturity and the Real Effects of the Panic of August 2007." *Critical Finance Review* Vol. 1, pp. 3-58.

[5] Almeida, Heitor, Murillo Campello, and Scott Weisbenner. 2004. "The Cash Flow Sensitivity of Cash" *Journal of Finance* Vol. 57(4), pp. 1777-1804.

[6] Barakova, Irina and Harini Parthasarathy. 2012. "How committed are bank corporate line commitments." *manuscript,* Washington, DC: Office of the Comptroller of the Currency.

[7] Berrospide, Jose M. 2013. "Bank Liquidity Hoarding and the Financial Crisis: An Empirical Evaluation." *Finance and Economics Discussion Series* 2013-3. Washington, DC: Board of Governors of the Federal Reserve System.

[8] Boot, Arnoud, Anjan V. Thakor, and Gregory F. Udell. 1987. "Competition, Risk Neutrality and Loan Commitments." *Journal of Banking and Finance* Vol. 11(3), pp. 449-471.

[9] Campello, Murillo, Erasmo Giambona, John R. Graham, and Campbell R. Harvey. 2011. "Liquidity Management and Corporate Investment during the Financial Crisis." *Review of Financial Studies* Vol. 24(6), pp. 1944-1979.

[10] Campello, Murillo, Erasmo Giambona, John R. Graham, and Campbell R. Harvey. 2012. "Access to Liquidity and Corporate Investment in Europe during the Financial Crisis." *Review of Finance* Vol. 16(2), pp. 323-346.

[11] Campello, Murillo, John R. Graham, and Campbell R. Harvey. 2010. "The Real Effects of Financing Constraints: Evidence from a Financial Crisis." *Journal of Financial Economics* Vol. 97(3), pp. 470-487.

[12] Chava, Sudheer and Michael R. Roberts. 2008. "How Does Financing Impact Investment? The Role of Debt Covenants." *Journal of Finance* Vol. 63(5), pp. 2085-2121.

[13] Chen, Zhaohui, Yan Hu, and Connie Mao. 2011. "How Much Liquidity Insurance can Lines of Credit Provide? The Impact of Bank Reputation and Lending Relationship." *manuscript.*

[14] Chodorow-Reich, Gabriel. 2014. 'The Employment Effects of Credit Market Disruptions: Firm-level Evidence from the 20089 Financial Crisis." *Quarterly Journal of Economics* Vol. 129(1), pp. 1-59.

[15] Cornett, Marcia M., Jamie J. McNutt, Philip E. Strahan, and Hassan Tehranian. 2011. "Liquidity Risk Management and Credit Supply in the Financial Crisis." *Journal of Financial Economics* Vol. 101(2), pp. 297-312.

[16] Demiroglu, Cem and Christopher M. James. 2011. "The Use of Bank Lines of Credit in Corporate Liquidity Management: A Review of Empirical Evidence." *Journal of Banking & Finance* Vol. 35(4), pp. 775-782.

[17] Demiroglu, Cem, Christopher M. James, and Atay Kizilaslan. 2009. "Credit Market Conditions and the Determinants and Value of Bank Lines of Credit for Private Firms." *manuscript,* Gainesville: University of Florida.

[18] Denis, David J. and Valeriy Sibilkov. 2010. "Financial Constraints, Investment, and the Value of Cash Holdings." *Review of Financial Studies* Vol. 23(1), pp. 247-269.

[19] Duchin, Ran, Oguzhan Ozbas, and Berk A. Sensoy. 2010. "Financial Constraints, Investment, and the Subprime Mortgage Crisis" *Journal of Financial Economics* Vol. 83, pp. 599-632.

[20] Falato, Antonio and J. Nellie Liang. 2014. "Do Creditor Rights Increase Employment Risk? Evidence from Loan Covenants." *Finance and Economics Discussion Series* 2014-61. Washington, DC: Board of Governors of the Federal Reserve System.

[21] Faulkender, Michael and Rong Wang. 2006 "Corporate Financial Policy and the Value of Cash" *Journal of Finance* Vol. 61(4), pp. 1975-1990.

[22] Gatev, Evan and Philip E. Strahan. 2006. "Banks' Advantage in Hedging Liquidity Risk: Theory and Evidence from the Commercial Paper Market." *Journal of Finance* Vol. 61(1), pp. 867-892.

[23] Holmström, Bengt and Jean Tirole. 2000. "Liquidity and Risk Management." *Journal of Money, Credit and Banking* Vol. 32(3), pp. 295-319.

[24] Huang, Rocco. 2010. "How Committed are Bank Lines of Credit? Experiences in the Subprime Mortgage Crisis." *manuscript,* East Lansing: Michigan State University.

[25] Ivashina, Victoria and David S. Scharfstein. 2010. "Bank Lending during the Financial Crisis of 2008." *Journal of Financial Economics* Vol. 97(3), pp. 319-338.

[26] Jiménez, Gabriel, Jose A. Lopez, and Jesús Saurina. 2009. "Empirical Analysis of Corporate Credit Lines." *Review of Financial Studies* Vol. 22(12), pp. 5069-5098.

[27] Kashyap, Anil K., Raghuram Rajan, and Jeremy C. Stein. 2002. "Banks as Liquidity Providers: An Explanation for the Coexistence of Lending and Deposit-taking." *Journal of Finance* Vol. 57(1), pp. 33-73.

[28] Lins, Karl V., Henri Servaes, and Peter Tufano. 2010. "What Drives Corporate Liquidity? An International Survey of Cash Holdings and Lines of Credit." *Journal of Financial Economics* Vol. 98(1), pp. 160-176.

[29] Mian, Atif and Joao A. C. Santos. 2011. "Liquidity Risk and Maturity Management over the Credit Cycle." *manuscript*, Berkeley: University of California.

[30] Montoriol-Garriga, Judit and Evan Sekeris. 2009. "A Question of Liquidity: The Great Banking Run of 2008?" *Federal Reserve Bank of Boston Working Paper* No. QAU09-4.

[31] Nini, Greg, David C. Smith, and Amir Sufi. 2010. "Creditor Control Rights and Firm Investment Policy." *Journal of Financial Economics* Vol. 92(3), pp. 400-420.

[32] Opler, Tim, Lee Pinkowitz, Rene Stulz, and Rohan Williamson. 1999. "The Determinants and Implications of Corporate Cash Holdings" *Journal of Financial Economics* Vol. 52(1), pp. 3-46.

[33] Rampini, Adriano and S. Viswanathan. 2010. "Collateral, Risk Management, and the Distribution of Debt Capacity." *Journal of Finance* Vol. 65(6), pp. 2293-2322.

[34] Santos. Joao A. C. 2010. "Bank corporate loan pricing following the subprime crisis." *Review of Financial Studies* Vol. 24(6), pp. 1919-1943.

[35] Shockley, Richard L. and Anjan V. Thakor. 1997. "Bank Loan Commitment Contracts: Data, Theory, and Tests." *Journal of Money, Credit and Banking* Vol. 29(4), pp. 517-534.

[36] Sufi, Amir. 2009. "Bank Lines of Credit in Corporate Finance: An Empirical Analysis." *Review of Financial Studies* Vol. 22(3), pp. 1057-1088.

[37] Sun, Qi. 2013. "Why does cash coexist with unused lines of credit? " University of Southern California. Working Paper.

[38] Thakor, Anjan V. 2005. "Do Loan Commitments Cause Overlending?" *Journal of Money, Credit and Banking* Vol. 36(6), pp. 1067-99.

[39] Tirole, Jean. 2006. *The Theory of Corporate Finance*. Princeton: Princeton University Press.

Appendix 1 - Data definitions and sources

Capital Expenditures (CAPEX)): Cash outflow or funds used for additions to firm's property, plant and equipment. Source: COMPUSTAT.

Cash: Sum of all cash and cash-like instruments. Source: COMPUSTAT.

Cashflow: Cash flow from operations. Source: COMPUSTAT.

CashFlow Volatility: Standard deviation of quarterly cash flow from operations over the previous 16 quarters. Source: COMPUSTAT.

Credit Line Availability: Amount of credit line that can be accessed. Note that availability can be lower than the total credit line because of covenant restrictions. Source: SEC filings.

Credit Line Availability Ratio: Credit line availability divided by total assets. Note that availability can be lower than the total credit line because of covenant restrictions. Source: SEC filings.

Credit Line Drawdown Size: The quarterly difference in the outstanding amount on the credit line divided by total assets. Source: SEC filings.

Credit Line Drawdown Dummy: The dummy is equal to 1 if the quarterly difference in the outstanding amount on the credit line is positive and 0 otherwise. Source: SEC filings.

Leverage: The sum of long term debt and debt in current liabilities divided by total assets. Source: COMPUSTAT.

Market-to-Book Ratio: The sum of market value of equity and book value of debt divided by total assets. Source: COMPUSTAT.

PPE: Sum of property, plant, and equipment plus depreciation. Source: COMPUSTAT.

Operating Income: Firm's income less all operating expenses. Source: COMPUSTAT.

Sales Growth: The quarterly growth in sales. Source: COMPUSTAT.

SLOOS: The net percentage of senior loan officers that report a tightening of lending standards in the Federal Reserve's Senior Loan Officer Opinion Survey. Source: Federal Reserve.

Tangible Assets: Total assets less intangible assets (goodwill, patents, blueprints, licences, etc.). Source: COMPUSTAT.

TED Spread: Difference between the three month London Interbank Offered Rate and the three month U.S. Treasury Rate. Source: Federal Reserve Economic Data (FRED).

Total Assets: Sum of assets. Source: COMPUSTAT.

Z-score: The modified Altman Z-score is the sum of 1.2*working capital, 1.4*retained earning, 3.3*EBIT and 0.999*sales, divided by total assets. Note that we use quarterly data except for EBIT, which is annual. We use last year's EBIT. The market-to-book ratio is included separately in the regressions and is therefore excluded here. Source: COMPUSTAT.

Appendix 2 - Credit Line Data taken from SEC regulatory Filings

This appendix serves two purposes. First, we illustrate, from a firm's perspective, the purposes of credit line usage. Second, we illustrate the credit line data collection process by considering a particular firm in 2006.

1. We illustrate through the following examples that credit lines are used, among other purposes, for investment financing (e.g., capital expenditures, acquisitions and/or merger financing, and working capital).

   - **Calumet Specialty Products**: "On March 31, 2006, the company financed the purchase of refinery equipment as part of a capacity expansion project at its Shreveport refinery through the borrowings under the revolving credit facility."

   - **Integra Lifesciences Holdings Corp.**: "On July 28, 2008 we borrowed $80 million under our senior revolving credit facility to fund the acquisition of Theken and for other general corporate purposes."

2. To illustrate the credit line data collection process, we consider the 2006 10-K filing of **Bernard Chaus Inc.**, which states the following: "The company has a financing agreement with CIT Group which provides a $40 million revolving line of credit with a $25 million sublimit for letters of credit, and a term loan for $10.5 million. On September 30, 2006, the company had $3.7 million of outstanding letters of credit under the Revolving Facility, total availability of approximately $20.2 million, a balance of $5.2 million on the term loan and $6.0 million in revolving credit borrowing."

   From this information on the company's credit line, we construct the following variables as of 2006:Q3:

   - Total Line = $50.5 million
   - Term Loan = $10.5 million
   - Total Revolving Line = $40.0 million
   - Used = $6.0 million
   - Unused = $34 million
   - Credit line availability = $20.2 (we use $26.2, which includes the used portion)

31

Table 1: Sample Summary Statistics

This table provides the summary statistics for our original random sample of 600 firms with credit lines. The unit of observation is a firm-quarter. All variables are defined in appendix 1.

Variable	N	Mean	Std. Dev.	Min.	25%	Median	75%	Max
Total Assets (in mill.)	11907	2955.12	11362.91	0.00	101.29	500.66	1867.10	212949.00
Total Revenue (in mill.)	11909	804.80	4604.83	0.00	21.59	114.32	428.08	113622.00
Debt/Assets	11588	0.23	0.25	0.00	0.01	0.17	0.35	1.36
Cash/Assets	11902	0.21	0.23	0.00	0.04	0.13	0.30	0.95
Net Income/Assets	11899	-0.01	0.08	-0.49	-0.01	0.01	0.02	0.11
Cash Flow/Assets	11546	-0.00	0.08	-0.48	0.00	0.02	0.03	0.11
Operating Margin/Assests	11540	0.01	0.07	-0.33	0.01	0.03	0.04	0.12
Tangible Assets/Assets	11900	0.82	0.19	0.24	0.71	0.89	0.99	1.00
Market-to-Book Ratio (Assets)	11308	2.03	1.42	0.62	1.17	1.57	2.31	8.00
Credit Line/Assets	11755	0.13	0.15	0.00	0.00	0.09	0.20	0.78
Credit Line Use/Assets	11680	0.04	0.17	0.00	0.00	0.00	0.03	10.48

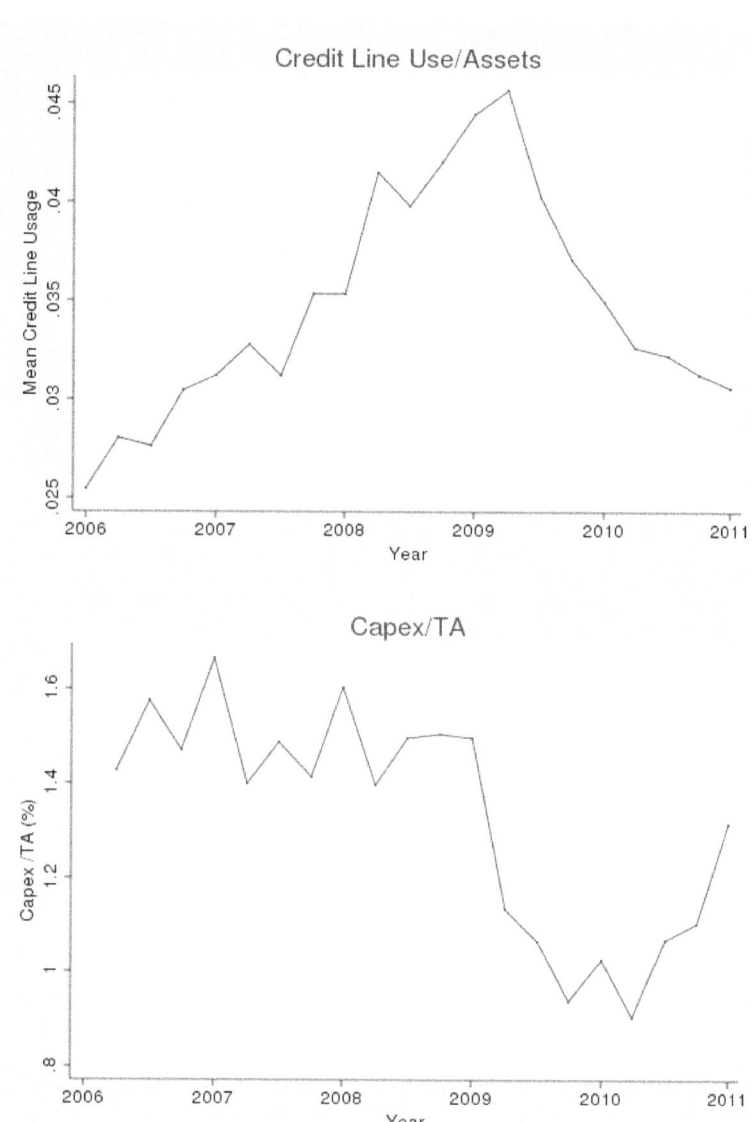

Figure 1: **Average Revolving Credit Line Use and Average Capital Expenditure.**
Credit line use is the average ratio of the amount of outstanding credit line balances to the firm's total assets for our sample of 467 firms. Capex is average quarterly capital expenditure divided by total assets. Outstanding credit lines balances are collected from SEC 10-Ks and 10-Qs. Capex and total assets are taken from COMPUSTAT.

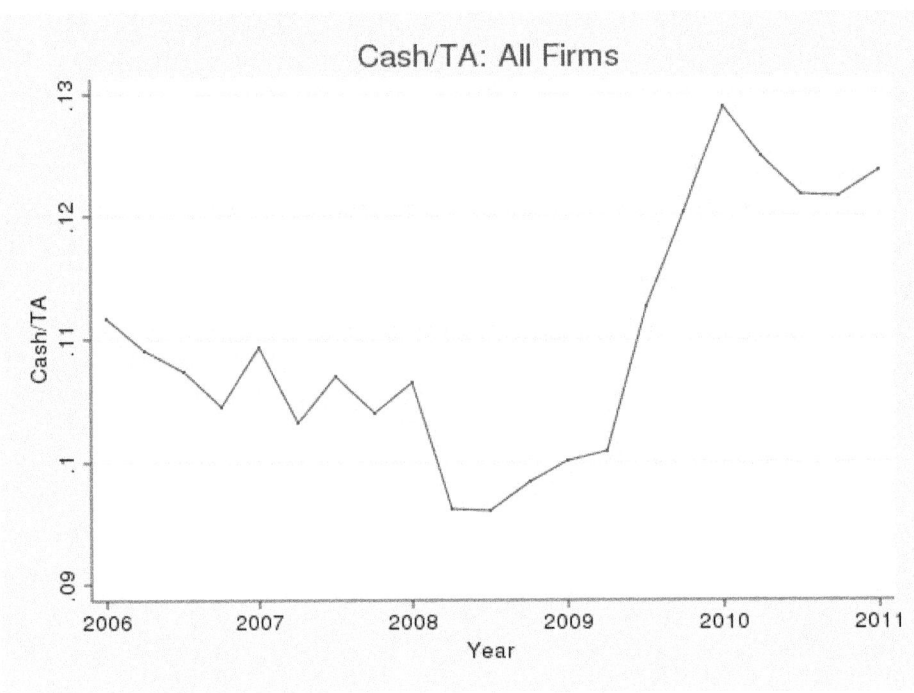

Figure 2: **Average Cash Holdings.**
Cash is the average ratio of the sum of cash and cash-like instruments to total assets for our sample of 467 firms. Cash and total assets are taken from COMPUSTAT.

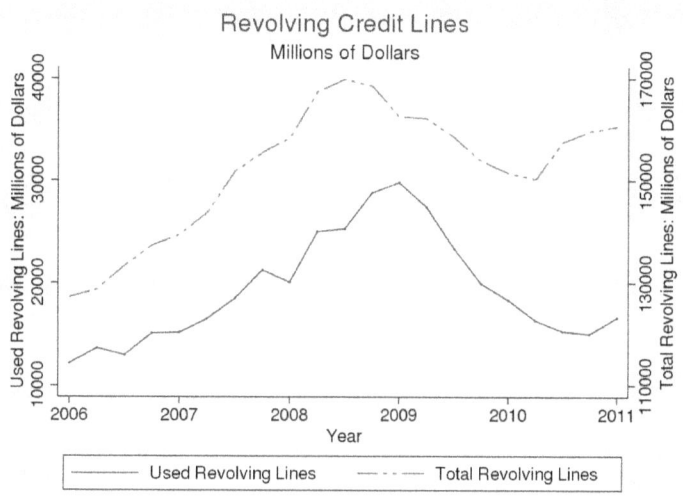

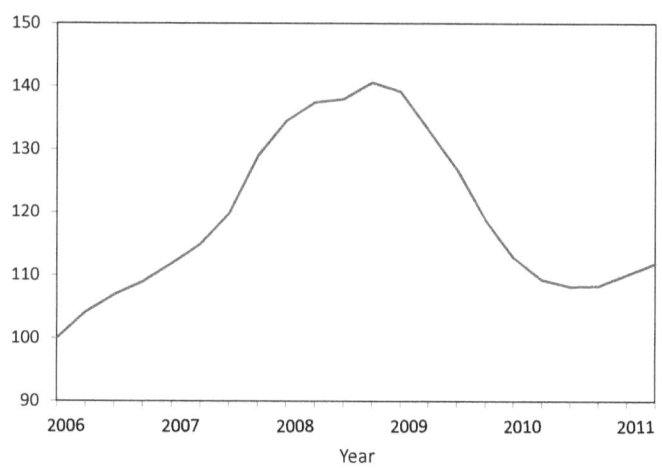

Figure 3: **Credit Lines and Bank C&I loans.**
Used revolving lines is the sum of outstanding credit line balances for our sample of 467 firms.
Total revolving lines is the sum of credit line size. Bank C&I loans is an index of total outstanding
loans to nonfinancial corporations normalized to the first quarter of 2006. Credit line information
is collected from SEC 10-Ks and 10-Qs. Bank C&I loans are aggregated across U.S. commercial
banks using Call Report data.

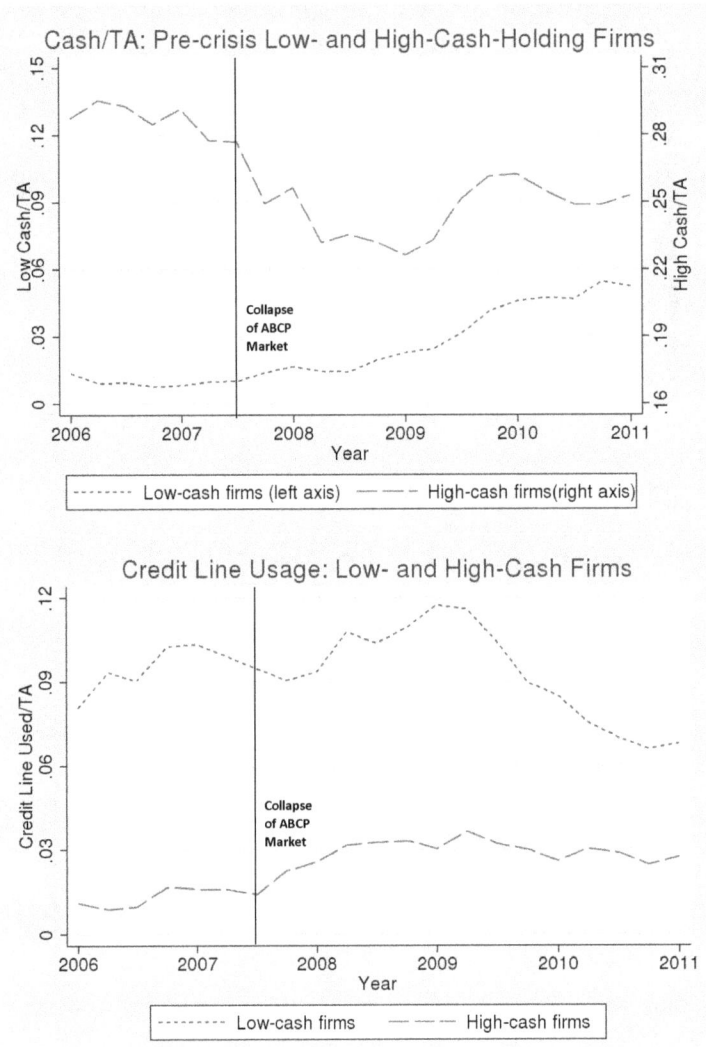

Figure 4: **Cash Holdings and Credit Line Usage by Cash Holdings.**
Cash is the average sum of cash and cash-like instruments divided by total assets for our sample of 467 firms. Credit line usage is the ratio of the amount of outstanding credit line balances to the firm's total assets. Low-cash firms are defined as having below average cash holdings between 2005:Q1 and 2007:Q1, and high-cash firms as having above average cash holdings over the same period. Outstanding credit lines balances are collected from SEC 10-Ks and 10-Qs. Cash and total assets are taken from COMPUSTAT.

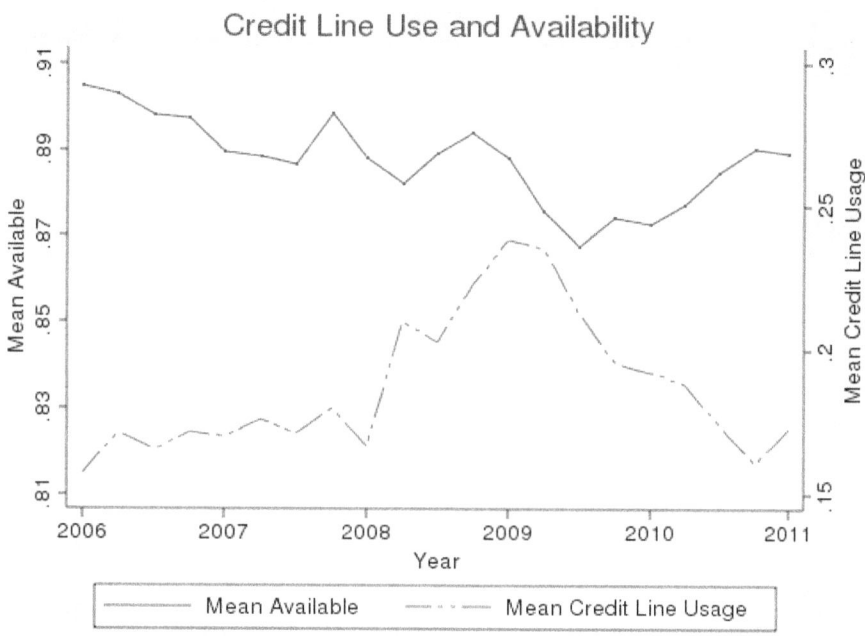

Figure 5: **Credit Lines Usage and Availability.**
Credit line use is the average ratio of the amount of credit line used to the total revolving line in our sample of 467 firms. Credit line availability is the fraction of credit line that can be accessed divided by the total revolving line. A detailed description is provided in appendix 1. Credit line information are collected from SEC 10-Ks and 10-Qs. Total assets are taken from COMPUSTAT.

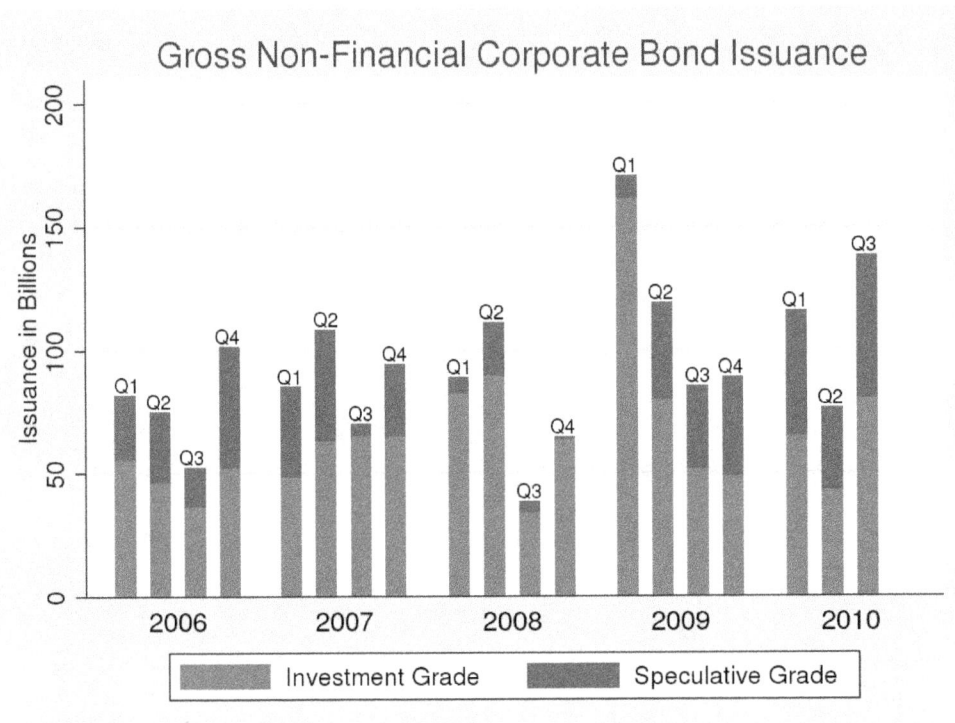

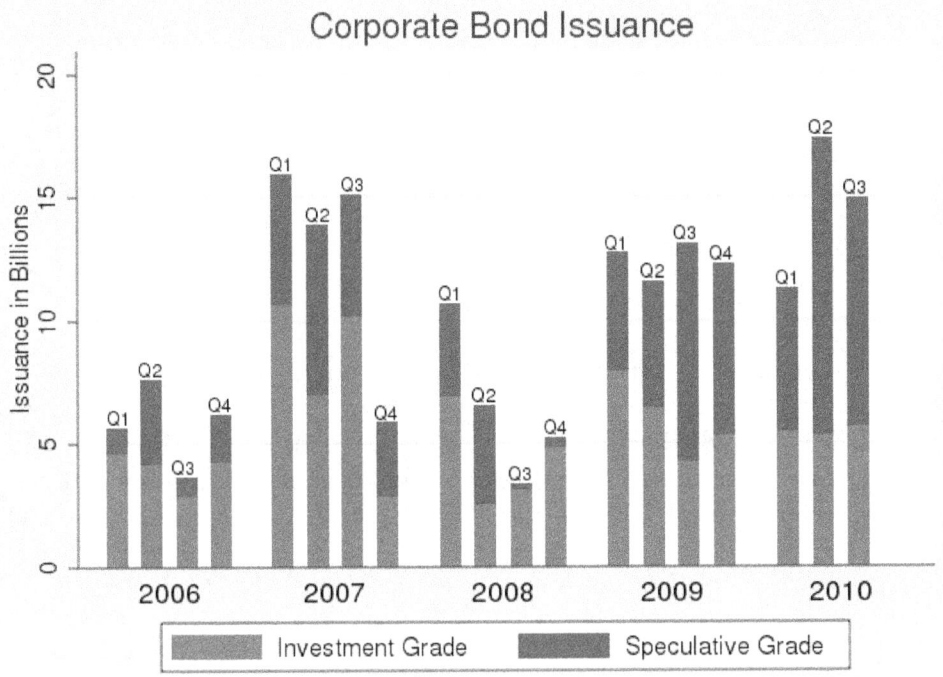

Figure 6: **All and Sample Corporate Bond Issuances.**
Corporate bond issuances are the total amount of bonds issued in each quarter. The top panel shows the overall bond market issuances and the bottom panel shows issuances by the 467 firms in our sample. Bond issuances are taken from Capital IQ.

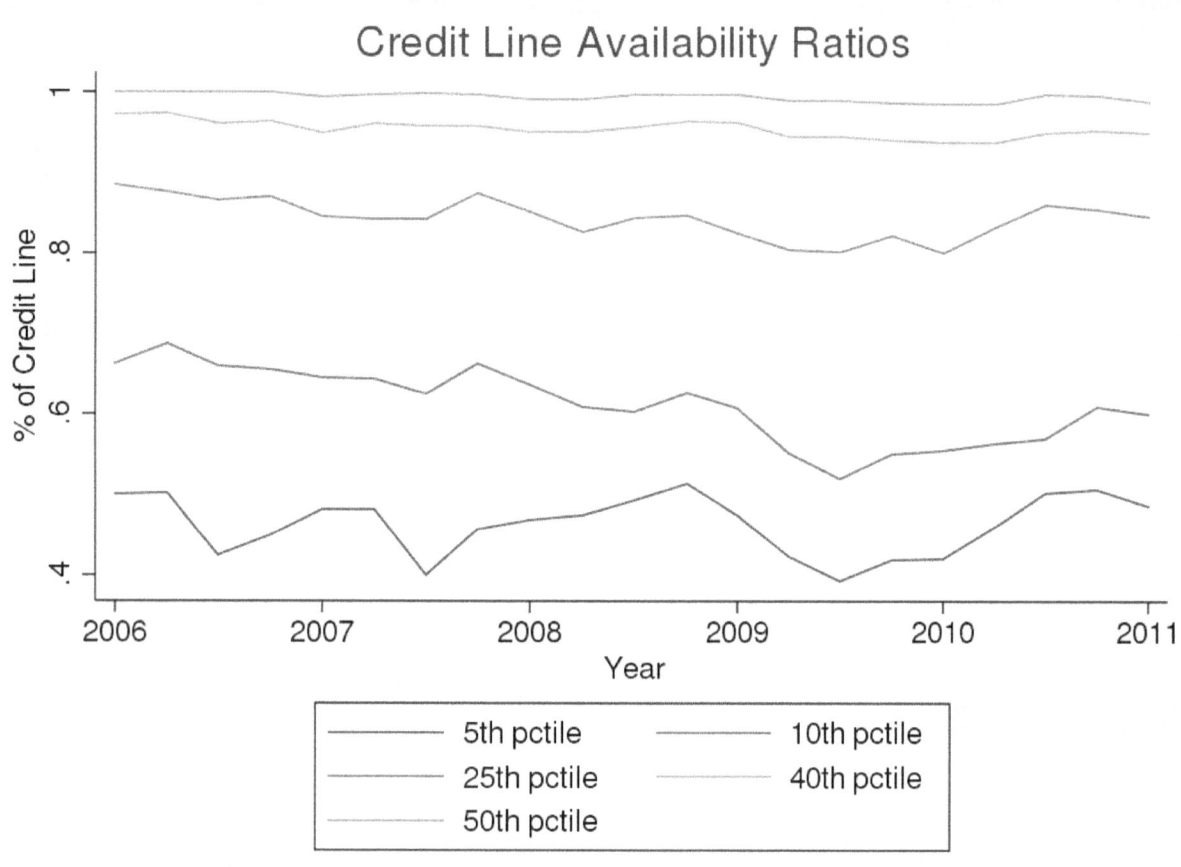

Figure 7: **Credit Line Availability by Percentile.**
Credit line availability is the fraction of the credit line that can be accessed divided by the credit line limit. A detailed description is provided in appendix 1. Credit line information is collected from SEC 10-Ks and 10-Qs.

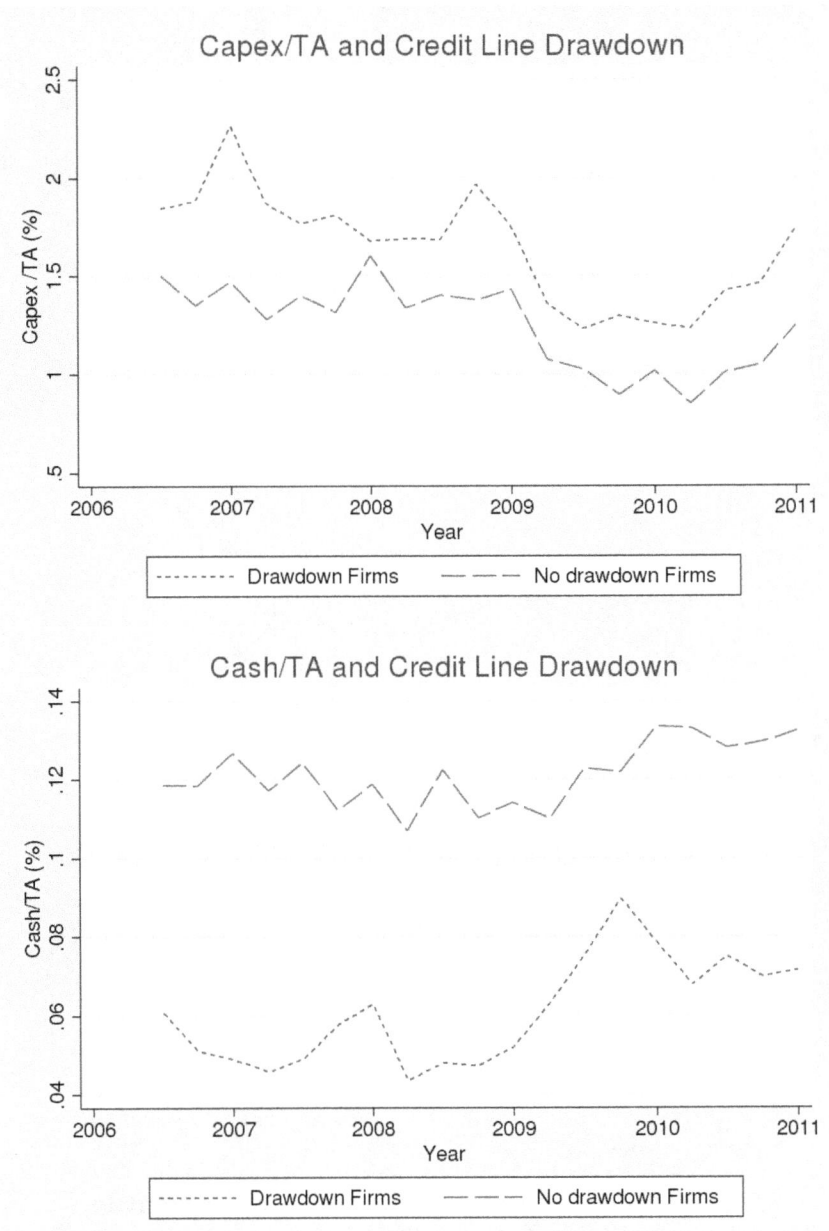

Figure 8: **Capital Expenditures and Cash Holdings by Credit Line Drawdown Status.**
Cash is the average sum of cash and cash-like instruments divided by total assets. Capex is average
quarterly capital expenditure divided by total assets. A "Drawdown Firm" is a firm that drew
on its credit line in the previous quarter. A "No drawdown Firm" did not draw on its credit line
in the previous quarter. Cash, capex, and total assets are taken from COMPUSTAT. Credit line
information is collected from SEC 10-Ks and 10-Qs.

40

Table 2: Summary Statistics of Regression Variables

This table provides the summary statistic for all regression variables used in the analysis (sample of 467 firms). The unit of observation is a firm-quarter. All variables are defined in appendix 1.

Variable	N	Mean	Std. Dev.	Min.	25%	Median	75%	Max
Cash/Assets	9471	0.143	0.155	0.000	0.029	0.090	0.210	0.951
Capex/Assets	9034	0.013	0.016	0.000	0.004	0.008	0.016	0.090
PPE/Assets	8727	0.015	0.020	-0.037	0.005	0.010	0.019	0.110
Credit Line/Assets	9420	0.168	0.154	0.000	0.065	0.128	0.231	0.779
Credit Line Use/Assets	9345	0.049	0.192	0.000	0.000	0.000	0.049	10.479
Drawdown dummy	8868	0.207	0.405	0.000	0.000	0.000	0.000	1.000
Drawdown/Assets	8860	0.001	0.027	-0.094	0.000	0.000	0.000	0.113
Log(assets)	9471	6.430	1.892	-0.257	5.064	6.528	7.730	12.269
Cash Flow/Assets	9192	0.011	0.063	-0.478	0.008	0.021	0.033	0.115
Operating Margin/Assets	9187	0.026	0.046	-0.335	0.016	0.031	0.045	0.121
Sales Growth	8949	0.030	0.222	-0.657	-0.054	0.018	0.088	1.859
Market-to-Book Ratio	8900	1.794	1.093	0.620	1.150	1.473	2.046	8.000
Tangible Assets/Assets	9469	0.800	0.200	0.240	0.681	0.868	0.972	1.000
Z-score	7504	1.110	3.241	-28.934	0.754	1.578	2.349	6.146
Cash Flow Volatility	8116	0.033	0.044	0.000	0.015	0.023	0.037	1.048
Leverage	9209	0.255	0.244	0.000	0.056	0.215	0.372	1.364
Available Credit Line/Assets	9340	0.105	0.100	0.000	0.038	0.083	0.146	1.000
Crisis Dummy	9480	0.293	0.455	0.000	0.000	0.000	1.000	1.000
SLOOS	9480	15.854	28.733	-12.300	-8.800	0.000	32.200	83.600
TED Spread	9480	69.206	54.609	13.021	36.667	60.667	92.542	255.917

Table 3: Regression Results: Drawdown Propensity and Drawdown Size

This table summarizes fixed effect logit panel regression results with a drawdown indicator at time t as the dependent variable, and fixed effect panel regressions with drawdown size at time t as the dependent variable. The drawdown indicator is equal to 1 if a firm drew on its credit line in the current quarter. Sales growth is measured as the quarterly change in sales divided by previous quarter sales. Crisis is a dummy variable equal to 1 for the 2007:Q3-2008:Q4 period. Additional controls are size (log of total assets), cash/assets, market-to-book ratio, tangible assets/assets, leverage, used credit line/available credit line as a measure of remaining debt capacity, a dummy variable for firms with market-to-book ratio greater than or equal to 8, cash flow volatility, and the inverse mills ratio. All variables are defined in appendix 1. All independent variables are lagged one period. We include time effects for each and every quarter.

| | Drawdown Propensity: Fixed Effect Logit Panel Regression | | | | | |
	(1)	(2)	(3)	(4)	(5)	(6)
Cashflow/TA	-2.295***			-2.272**		
	(0.831)			(0.893)		
Cashflow/TA*Crisis				-0.087		
				(1.226)		
Oper. Inc./TA		-3.452**			-2.672*	
		(1.457)			(1.496)	
Oper. Inc./TA*Crisis					-3.583**	
					(1.752)	
Sales Growth			-0.521***			-0.315
			(0.180)			(0.221)
Sales Growth*Crisis						-0.568
						(0.376)
Controls	yes	yes	yes	yes	yes	yes
Firm Fixed Effects	yes	yes	yes	yes	yes	yes
Time Effects	yes	yes	yes	no	yes	yes
No. Obs	4957	4953	4933	4957	4953	4933
Chi^2	332.9	330.5	334.4	332.9	334.8	336.7

	Drawdown Size: Fixed Effect Panel Regression					
Cashflow/TA	-0.017*			-0.007		
	(0.010)			(0.011)		
Cashflow/TA*Crisis				-0.042**		
				(0.020)		
Oper. Inc./TA		-0.041**			-0.028	
		(0.019)			(0.019)	
Oper. Inc./TA*Crisis					-0.058**	
					(0.026)	
Sales Growth			-0.008***			-0.005**
			(0.002)			(0.002)
Sales Growth*Crisis						-0.007*
						(0.004)
Controls	yes	yes	yes	yes	yes	yes
Firm Fixed Effects	yes	yes	yes	yes	yes	yes
Time Effects	yes	yes	yes	no	yes	yes
No. Obs	7069	7064	7078	7069	7064	7078
Adjusted R^2	.0378477	.0380676	.0364413	.0397436	.0401669	.036966

Standard errors in parentheses. * $p < 0.10$, ** $p < 0.05$, *** $p < 0.01$.

Table 4: Regression Results: Capital Expenditures

This table summarizes fixed effect panel regression results with capital expenditure at time t as the dependent variable. Capital expenditure is measured as the ratio of capital expenditures to total assets. Crisis is a dummy variable that is equal to 1 for the 2007:Q3-2008:Q4 period. Size is measured as the natural log of total assess, and MTB is market-to-book ratio. We also include a dummy variable for firms with market-to-book ratio greater than or equal to 8. Instruments are described in the main text. All variables are defined in appendix 1. All independent variables are lagged one period. We include time effects for each and every quarter.

	FE Panel Regression		FE Panel IV Regression	
	(1)	(2)	(3)	(4)
Drawdown	0.019***	0.021***	0.044*	0.036
	(0.005)	(0.006)	(0.024)	(0.024)
Drawdown*Crisis		-0.003		0.039***
		(0.010)		(0.009)
Sales Growth	0.001	0.001	0.000	0.000
	(0.001)	(0.001)	(0.001)	(0.001)
Oper. Inc./TA	-0.002	-0.002	0.004	0.003
	(0.009)	(0.009)	(0.010)	(0.010)
Cash/TA	0.003	0.003	0.005*	0.005*
	(0.002)	(0.002)	(0.003)	(0.003)
Size	-0.004***	-0.004***	-0.003***	-0.003***
	(0.001)	(0.001)	(0.001)	(0.001)
Tangible Assets/TA	-0.003	-0.003	-0.006**	-0.005*
	(0.003)	(0.003)	(0.003)	(0.003)
MTB ratio	0.002***	0.002***	0.003***	0.003***
	(0.000)	(0.000)	(0.000)	(0.000)
MTB > 8 Dummy	-0.008***	-0.008***	-0.016***	-0.016***
	(0.003)	(0.003)	(0.003)	(0.003)
Leverage	-0.005**	-0.005**	-0.008***	-0.008***
	(0.002)	(0.002)	(0.002)	(0.002)
Zscore	0.000*	0.000*	0.000	0.000
	(0.000)	(0.000)	(0.000)	(0.000)
Cash-Flow Volatility	0.008	0.008	0.021	0.021
	(0.015)	(0.015)	(0.015)	(0.015)
Inv. Mills ratio	0.159	0.160	0.256*	0.270*
	(0.116)	(0.116)	(0.150)	(0.150)
Firm Fixed Effects	yes	yes	yes	yes
Time Effects	yes	yes	yes	yes
No. Obs	6610	6610	6000	6000
Adjusted R^2	.68	.68	.69	.69

Standard errors in parentheses. * $p < 0.10$, ** $p < 0.05$, *** $p < 0.01$.

Table 5: Cross Section Regression Results: Capital Expenditures

This table summarizes cross-sectional regression results with cumulative capital expenditure during the crisis period (2007:Q3-2008:Q3) as the dependent variable. Capital expenditure is measured as the ratio of capital expenditures to total assets. All regressions include the following additional controls: size (log assets), sales growth, operating income/assets, cash/assets, market-to-book ratio, tangible assets/assets, leverage, a dummy variable for firms with market-to-book ratio greater than or equal to 8, and cash flow volatility. Instruments are described in the main text. All variables are defined in appendix 1. All independent variables are averaged over the 2005:Q4-2007:Q2 period.

	OLS Capex (1)	First Stage Drawdown (2)	IV Capex (3)
Drawdown	0.282***		0.695**
	(0.056)		(0.327)
Pre-Crisis Availability		0.112**	
		(0.053)	
Controls	yes	yes	yes
No. Obs	424	419	419
Adjusted R^2	.27	.054	.23

Robust standard errors in parentheses. * $p < 0.10$, ** $p < 0.05$, *** $p < 0.01$.

Table 6: Capital Expenditures Regression with Additional Lags

This table summarizes fixed effect panel regression results with capital expenditure at time t as the dependent variable. Capital expenditure is measured as the ratio of capital expenditures to total assets. Crisis is a dummy variable that is equal to 1 for the 2007:Q3-2008:Q4 period. All regressions include the following additional controls: size (log assets), sales growth, operating income/assets, cash/assets, market-to-book ratio, tangible assets/assets, leverage, market-to-book ratio greater than or equal to 8 dummy, cash flow volatility, and the inverse mills ratio. Instruments are described in the main text. Four lags of additional control variables, except cash flow volatility, are included. All variables are defined in appendix 1. We also include time effects for each and every quarter.

	FE Panel Regression		FE Panel IV Regression	
	(1)	(2)	(3)	(4)
Drawdown	0.013**	0.013*	0.064**	0.052*
	(0.005)	(0.007)	(0.028)	(0.028)
Drawdown*Crisis		-0.001		0.042***
		(0.010)		(0.010)
Controls	yes	yes	yes	yes
Firm Fixed Effects	yes	yes	yes	yes
Time Effects	yes	yes	yes	yes
No. Obs	5612	5612	5123	5123
Adjusted R^2	.70	.70	.71	.71

Standard errors in parentheses. * $p < 0.10$, ** $p < 0.05$, *** $p < 0.01$.

Table 7: Robustness: Investment in PPE / Total Assets

This table summarizes fixed effect panel regression results with investment at time t as the dependent variable. Investment is measured as the ratio of the change in PPE to total assets. Crisis is a dummy variable that is equal to 1 for the 2007:Q3-2008:Q4 period. All regressions include the following additional controls: size (log assets), sales growth, operating income/assets, cash/assets, market-to-book ratio, tangible assets/assets, leverage, a dummy variable for firms with market-to-book ratio greater than or equal to 8, cash flow volatility, and the inverse mills ratio. Instruments are described in the main text. All variables are defined in appendix 1. All independent variables are lagged one period. We include time effects for each and every quarter.

	FE Panel Regression		FE Panel IV Regression	
	(1)	(2)	(3)	(4)
Drawdown	0.003	0.004	0.091**	0.088**
	(0.009)	(0.011)	(0.042)	(0.043)
Drawdown*Crisis		-0.004		0.013
		(0.018)		(0.015)
Controls	yes	yes	yes	yes
Firm Fixed Effects	yes	yes	yes	yes
Time Effects	yes	yes	yes	yes
No. Obs	6611	6611	6000	6000
Adjusted R^2	.40	.40	.41	.41
log(likelihood)	18400	18400	16787	16788

Standard errors in parentheses. * $p < 0.10$, ** $p < 0.05$, *** $p < 0.01$.

Table 8: Robustness: Capital Expenditure Regressions with Macro Variables

This table summarizes fixed effect panel regression results with capital expenditure at time t as the dependent variable. Capital expenditure is measured as the ratio of capital expenditures to total assets. The TED spread is defined as LIBOR minus the Treasury rate of similar maturity. SLOOS, measuring banks' willingness to lend, is taken from the Federal Reserve's Senior Loan Officer Opinion Survey. All regressions include the following additional controls: size (log of assets), sales growth, operating income/assets, cash/assets, market-to-book ratio, tangible assets/assets, leverage, a dummy variable for firms with market-to-book ratio greater than or equal to 8, cash flow volatility, and the inverse mills ratio. Instruments are described in the main text. All variables are defined in appendix 1. All independent variables are lagged one period. We include time effects for each and every quarter.

	FE Panel Regression		FE Panel IV Regression	
	(1)	(2)	(3)	(4)
Drawdown	0.022***	0.020***	0.034	0.040*
	(0.008)	(0.006)	(0.024)	(0.024)
Drawdown*TED	-0.003		0.018**	
	(0.009)		(0.007)	
Drawdown*SLOOS		-0.002		0.043***
		(0.016)		(0.014)
Controls	yes	yes	yes	yes
Firm Fixed Effects	yes	yes	yes	yes
Time Effects	yes	yes	yes	yes
No. Obs	6610	6610	6000	6000
Adjusted R^2	.68	.68	.69	.69

Standard errors in parentheses. * $p < 0.10$, ** $p < 0.05$, *** $p < 0.01$.
^{a} TED and SLOOS coefficients multiplied by 100.

Table 9: Regression Results: Capital Expenditure by Dividend Status

This table summarizes fixed effect panel regression results with capital expenditure at time t as the dependent variable. Capital expenditure is measured as the ratio of capital expenditures to total assets. Crisis is a dummy variable that is equal to 1 for the 2007:Q3-2008:Q4 period. All regressions include the following additional controls: size (log assets), sales growth, operating income/assets, cash/assets, market-to-book ratio, tangible assets/assets, leverage, a dummy variable for firms with market-to-book ratio greater than or equal to 8, cash flow volatility, and the inverse mills ratio. Instruments are described in the main text. All variables are defined in appendix 1. All independent variables are lagged one period. We include time effects for each and every quarter.

	FE Panel Regression		FE Panel IV Regression	
	(1)	(2)	(3)	(4)
	Never Paid Dividends			
Drawdown	0.017**	0.016*	0.029	0.017
	(0.007)	(0.009)	(0.036)	(0.037)
Drawdown*Crisis		0.003		0.061***
		(0.014)		(0.016)
Controls	yes	yes	yes	yes
Firm Fixed Effects	yes	yes	yes	yes
Time Effects	yes	yes	yes	yes
No. Obs	3165	3165	2689	2689
Adjusted R^2	.67	.67	.68	.68
	Paid Dividends			
Drawdown	0.022***	0.026***	0.062**	0.054**
	(0.007)	(0.008)	(0.026)	(0.026)
Drawdown*Crisis		-0.009		0.028**
		(0.013)		(0.012)
Controls	yes	yes	yes	yes
Firm Fixed Effects	yes	yes	yes	yes
Time Effects	yes	yes	yes	yes
No. Obs	3445	3445	3311	3311
Adjusted R^2	.69	.69	.70	.70

Standard errors in parentheses. * $p < 0.10$, ** $p < 0.05$, *** $p < 0.01$.

Table 10: Regression Results: Capital Expenditures by Firm Size

This table summarizes fixed effect panel regression results with capital expenditure at time t as the dependent variable. Capital expenditure is measured as the ratio of capital expenditures to total assets. Small and large firms are those in the lower and upper tercile of the size distribution, respectively. Crisis is a dummy variable that is equal to 1 for the 2007:Q3-2008:Q4 period. Size is measured as the natural log of total assets, and MTB is market-to-book ratio. We include time effects for each and every quarter. We also include a dummy variable for firms with market-to-book ratio greater than or equal to 8. Instruments are described in the main text. All variables are defined in appendix 1. All independent variables are lagged one period.

	FE Panel Regression		FE Panel IV Regression	
	(1)	(2)	(3)	(4)
	Small Firms			
Drawdown	-0.001	0.004	-0.019	-0.029
	(0.006)	(0.007)	(0.028)	(0.029)
Drawdown*Crisis		-0.012		0.043*
		(0.013)		(0.022)
Controls	yes	yes	yes	yes
Firm Fixed Effects	yes	yes	yes	yes
Time Effects	yes	yes	yes	yes
No. Obs	1839	1839	1547	1547
Ajusted R^2	.51	.51	.50	.51
	Large Firms			
Drawdown	0.032***	0.028**	0.062*	0.055*
	(0.010)	(0.013)	(0.032)	(0.033)
Drawdown*Crisis		0.009		0.026
		(0.021)		(0.022)
Controls	yes	yes	yes	yes
Firm Fixed Effects	yes	yes	yes	yes
Time Effects	yes	yes	yes	yes
No. Obs	2550	2550	2433	2433
Ajusted R^2	.76	.76	.76	.76

Standard errors in parentheses. * $p < 0.10$, ** $p < 0.05$, *** $p < 0.01$.

Table 11: Regression Results: Capital Expenditures by firm Credit Rating

This table summarizes fixed effect panel regression results with capital expenditure at time t as the dependent variable. Capital expenditure is measured as the ratio of capital expenditures to total assets. Crisis is a dummy variable that is equal to 1 for the 2007:Q3-2008:Q4 period. Size is measured as the natural log of total assets, and MTB is market-to-book ratio. We include time effects for each and every quarter. We also include a dummy variable for firms with market-to-book ratio greater than or equal to 8. Instruments are described in the main text. All variables are defined in appendix 1. All independent variables are lagged one period.

	FE Panel Regression		FE Panel IV Regression	
	(1)	(2)	(3)	(4)
	Investment Grade			
Drawdown	0.010	0.031*	0.079	0.078
	(0.012)	(0.018)	(0.055)	(0.055)
Drawdown*Crisis		-0.044*		0.007
		(0.024)		(0.019)
Controls	yes	yes	yes	yes
Firm Fixed Effects	yes	yes	yes	yes
Time Effects	yes	yes	yes	yes
No. Obs	899	899	861	861
Adjusted R^2	.81	.81	.82	.82
	High yield			
Drawdown	0.031**	0.034**	0.114***	0.094**
	(0.012)	(0.016)	(0.037)	(0.037)
Drawdown*Crisis		-0.007		0.075**
		(0.024)		(0.034)
Controls	yes	yes	yes	yes
Firm Fixed Effects	yes	yes	yes	yes
Time Effects	yes	yes	yes	yes
No. Obs	1424	1424	1347	1347
Adjusted R^2	.70	.70	.70	.70
	No Rating			
Drawdown	0.016***	0.014**	0.035	0.021
	(0.006)	(0.007)	(0.029)	(0.029)
Drawdown*Crisis		0.004		0.060***
		(0.011)		(0.014)
Controls	yes	yes	yes	yes
Firm Fixed Effects	yes	yes	yes	yes
Time Effects	yes	yes	yes	yes
No. Obs	4287	4287	3792	3792
Adjusted R^2	.66	.66	.66	.66

Standard errors in parentheses. * $p < 0.10$, ** $p < 0.05$, *** $p < 0.01$.

Table 12: Regression Results: Cash Holding

This table summarizes fixed effect panel regression results with the cash-to-total assets ratio at time t as the dependent variable. Crisis is a dummy variable that is equal to 1 for the 2007:Q3-2008:Q4 period. Size is measured as the natural log of total assets, and MTB is market-to-book ratio. We include time effects for each and every quarter. We also include a dummy variable for firms with market-to-book ratio greater than or equal to 8. Instruments are described in the main text. All variables are defined in appendix 1.All independent variables are lagged one period.

	FE Panel Regression		FE Panel IV Regression	
	(1)	(2)	(3)	(4)
Drawdown	-0.012	-0.009	-0.348**	-0.383**
	(0.029)	(0.041)	(0.164)	(0.165)
Drawdown*Crisis		-0.009		0.158***
		(0.056)		(0.055)
Sales Growth	-0.007	-0.007	0.001	0.001
	(0.007)	(0.007)	(0.006)	(0.006)
Oper. Inc./TA	0.131***	0.131***	0.064	0.060
	(0.050)	(0.050)	(0.048)	(0.048)
Size	0.013**	0.013**	-0.002	-0.002
	(0.006)	(0.006)	(0.006)	(0.006)
Tangible Assets/TA	0.403***	0.403***	0.298***	0.298***
	(0.027)	(0.027)	(0.020)	(0.020)
MTB ratio	0.000	0.000	-0.003	-0.003
	(0.003)	(0.003)	(0.004)	(0.004)
MTB > 8 Dummy	0.053*	0.053*	0.075*	0.075*
	(0.029)	(0.029)	(0.040)	(0.040)
Leverage	-0.071***	-0.071***	-0.043***	-0.042***
	(0.016)	(0.016)	(0.015)	(0.015)
Zscore	0.005**	0.005**	0.015***	0.015***
	(0.002)	(0.002)	(0.002)	(0.002)
Cash-Flow Volatility	0.010	0.010	0.114	0.117
	(0.141)	(0.141)	(0.145)	(0.145)
Inv. Mills ratio	0.382	0.385	-1.082	-1.021
	(1.638)	(1.636)	(1.194)	(1.197)
Firm Fixed Effects	yes	yes	yes	yes
Time Effects	yes	yes	yes	yes
No. Obs	6611	6611	6000	6000
Adjusted R^2	.82	.82	.82	.82

Standard errors in parentheses. * $p < 0.10$, ** $p < 0.05$, *** $p < 0.01$.

Table 13: Cross Section Regression Results: Cash Holdings

This table summarizes cross-sectional regression results with cumulative cash holding changes during the crisis period (2007:Q3-2008:Q3) as the dependent variable. Cash is measured as the ratio of cash to total assets. All regressions include the following additional controls: size (log of assets), sales growth, operating income/assets, cash/assets, market-to-book ratio, tangible assets/assets, leverage, a dummy variable for firms with market-to-book ratio greater than or equal to 8, and cash flow volatility. Instruments are described in the main text. All variables are defined in appendix 1. All independent variables are averaged over the 2005:Q4-2007:Q2 period.

	OLS Cash (1)	First Stage Drawdown (2)	IV Cash (3)
Drawdown	-0.563**		-5.412***
	(0.266)		(1.491)
Pre-Crisis Availability		0.112**	
		(0.053)	
Controls	yes	yes	yes
No. Obs	424	419	419
Adjusted R^2	.24	.054	.26

Robust standard errors in parentheses. * $p < 0.10$, ** $p < 0.05$, *** $p < 0.01$.

Table 14: Robustness: Cash Holdings Regressions with Macro Variables

This table summarizes fixed effect panel regression results with cash holdings at time t as the dependent variable. Cash holdings is measured as the ratio of cash to total assets. The TED spread is defined as LIBOR minus the Treasury rate of similar maturity. SLOOS, measuring banks' willingness to lend, is taken from the Federal Reserve's Senior Loan Officer Opinion Survey. All regressions include the following additional controls: size (log assets), sales growth, operating income/assets, cash/assets, market-to-book ratio, tangible assets/assets, leverage, a dummy variable for firms with market-to-book ratio greater than or equal to 8, cash flow volatility, and the inverse mills ratio. Instruments are described in the main text. All variables are defined in appendix 1. All independent variables are lagged one period. We include time effects for each and every quarter.

	FE Panel Regression		FE Panel IV Regression	
	(1)	(2)	(3)	(4)
Drawdown	0.007	-0.007	-0.226	-0.196
	(0.042)	(0.033)	(0.142)	(0.140)
Drawdown*TED	-0.001		0.057	
	(0.042)		(0.036)	
Drawdown*SLOOS		0.058		0.031
		(0.098)		(0.076)
Controls	yes	yes	yes	yes
Firm Fixed Effects	yes	yes	yes	yes
Time Effects	yes	yes	yes	yes
No. Obs	6610	6610	6000	6000
Adjusted R^2	.68	.68	.69	.69

Standard errors in parentheses. * $p < 0.10$, ** $p < 0.05$, *** $p < 0.01$.
[a] TED and SLOOS coefficients multiplied by 100.

Table 15: Regression Results: Cash Holding by Dividend Status

This table summarizes fixed effect panel regression results with the cash-to-total assets ratio at time t as the dependent variable. Crisis is a dummy variable that is equal to 1 for the 2007:Q3-2008:Q4 period. All regressions include the following additional controls: size (log of assets), sales growth, operating income/assets, market-to-book ratio, tangible assets/assets, leverage, a dummy variable for firms with market-to-book ratio greater than or equal to 8, cash flow volatility, and the inverse mills ratio. Instruments are described in the main text. All variables are defined in appendix 1. All independent variables are lagged one period. We include time effects for each and every quarter.

	FE Panel Regression		FE Panel IV Regression	
	(1)	(2)	(3)	(4)
	Never Paid Dividends			
Drawdown	-0.018	-0.003	-0.396*	-0.402*
	(0.042)	(0.058)	(0.227)	(0.229)
Drawdown*Crisis		-0.039		0.031
		(0.082)		(0.082)
Controls	yes	yes	yes	yes
Firm Fixed Effects	yes	yes	yes	yes
Time Effects	yes	yes	yes	yes
No. Obs	3166	3166	2689	2689
Adjusted R^2	.88	.88	.87	.87
	Paid Dividends			
Drawdown	0.036	-0.004	0.161*	0.138
	(0.029)	(0.037)	(0.097)	(0.098)
Drawdown*Crisis		0.097*		0.077
		(0.056)		(0.056)
Controls	yes	yes	yes	yes
Firm Fixed Effects	yes	yes	yes	yes
Time Effects	yes	yes	yes	yes
No. Obs	3445	3445	3311	3311
Adjusted R^2	.90	.90	.89	.89
log(likelihood)	6537	6538	6488	6489

Standard errors in parentheses. * $p < 0.10$, ** $p < 0.05$, *** $p < 0.01$.

Table 16: Regression Results: Cash Holding by Firm Size

This table summarizes fixed effect panel regression results with the cash-to-total assets ratio at time t as the dependent variable. Small and large firms are those in the lower and upper tercile of the size distribution, respectively. Crisis is a dummy variable that is equal to 1 for the 2007:Q3-2008:Q4 period. Size is measured as the natural log of total assets, and MTB is market-to-book ratio. We also include a dummy variable for firms with market-to-book ratio greater than or equal to 8. Instruments are described in the main text. All variables are defined in appendix 1. All independent variables are lagged one period. We include time effects for each and every quarter.

	FE Panel Regression		FE Panel IV Regression	
	(1)	(2)	(3)	(4)
	Small Firms			
Drawdown	0.115*	0.080	-0.487*	-0.547*
	(0.059)	(0.081)	(0.275)	(0.288)
Drawdown*Crisis		0.087		0.266
		(0.106)		(0.180)
Controls	yes	yes	yes	yes
Firm Fixed Effects	yes	yes	yes	yes
Time Effects	yes	yes	yes	yes
No. Obs	1840	1840	1547	1547
Adjusted R^2	.88	.88	.88	.88
	Large Firms			
Drawdown	-0.027	-0.034	0.215**	0.185**
	(0.022)	(0.031)	(0.090)	(0.089)
Drawdown*Crisis		0.019		0.118
		(0.044)		(0.093)
Controls	yes	yes	yes	yes
Firm Fixed Effects	yes	yes	yes	yes
Time Effects	yes	yes	yes	yes
No. Obs	2550	2550	2433	2433
Adjusted R^2	.90	.90	.87	.89

Standard errors in parentheses. * $p < 0.10$, ** $p < 0.05$, *** $p < 0.01$.

Table 17: Regression Results: Cash Holding by firm Credit Rating

This table summarizes fixed effect panel regression results with the cash-to-total assets ratio at time t as the dependent variable. Crisis is a dummy variable that is equal to 1 for the 2007:Q3-2008:Q4 period. Size is measured as the natural log of total assets, and MTB is market-to-book ratio. We also include a dummy variable for firms with market-to-book ratio greater than or equal to 8. Instruments are described in the main text. All variables are defined in appendix 1. All independent variables are lagged one period. We include time effects for each and every quarter.

	FE Panel Regression		FE Panel IV Regression	
	(1)	(2)	(3)	(4)
	Investment Grade			
Drawdown	0.064*	0.052	0.420**	0.383**
	(0.036)	(0.049)	(0.181)	(0.184)
Drawdown*Crisis		0.025		0.228*
		(0.076)		(0.121)
Controls	yes	yes	yes	yes
Firm Fixed Effects	yes	yes	yes	yes
Time Effects	yes	yes	yes	yes
No. Obs	899	899	861	861
Adjusted R^2	.95	.95	.90	.90
	Non-Inv Grade			
Drawdown	-0.021	-0.002	0.063	0.037
	(0.030)	(0.042)	(0.125)	(0.130)
Drawdown*Crisis		-0.051		0.095
		(0.059)		(0.113)
Controls	yes	yes	yes	yes
Firm Fixed Effects	yes	yes	yes	yes
Time Effects	yes	yes	yes	yes
No. Obs	1424	1424	1347	1347
Adjusted R^2	.85	.85	.83	.83
	No Rating			
Drawdown	0.013	-0.004	-0.306*	-0.334*
	(0.036)	(0.049)	(0.177)	(0.180)
Drawdown*Crisis		0.040		0.122
		(0.071)		(0.077)
Controls	yes	yes	yes	yes
Firm Fixed Effects	yes	yes	yes	yes
Time Effects	yes	yes	yes	yes
No. Obs	4288	4288	3792	3792
Adjusted R^2	.88	.88	.88	.88

Standard errors in parentheses. * $p < 0.10$, ** $p < 0.05$, *** $p < 0.01$.